How We Used To Live 1851-1901

by Freda Kelsall

To provide a wide historical background to Yorkshire Television's new series *How We Used To Live, 1874-87*, this book deals with the whole of the later Victorian era, from 1851-1901.

Contents

Cover picture: a bank holiday beach scene in 1892 (Radio Times Hulton Picture Library).

Historical Adviser:
Norman Longmate
Editor: Tim Healey
Managing Editor: Anne Furniss
Production: Philip Hughes
Picture Research: Jenny De Gex

A MACDONALD BOOK

©Macdonald Educational Ltd 1978

First published in Great Britain in 1978
Reprinted in 1979, 1980, 1983, 1986

All rights reserved

ISBN 0 356 05935 9 (cased)
ISBN 0 356 05936 7 (limp)

Printed and bound in Great Britain by
Purnell Book Production Ltd
Paulton, Bristol

Published by
Macdonald & Company (Publishers) Ltd
Greater London House
Hampstead Road
London NW1 7QX

Members of BPCC plc

Acknowledgements

We wish to thank the following organizations and individuals for their assistance, and for making available material in their collections.

Author's collection, 54(L) (R)
Aberdeen Public Library/Batsford, 4(T)
Batsford, 23 (BL), 27 (B), 32 (BL), 33 (TL) (TR) (BR), 39 (TR), 41 (T), 45 (TL), 60 (L), 61 (BL)
Beamish Open Air Museum, 6 (TR), 33 (BC), 61 (BR); Beamish Open Air Museum/Batsford, 31 (CL)
City Art Gallery, Manchester, 8, 18, 26
Clydebank Public Library/Batsford, 39 (TL)
Crown Copyright, Victoria and Albert Museum, 27 (TL), 56 (R)
Mary Evans Picture Library, 6 (T) (BL), 17 (B), 21 (T), 32 (TL), 34 (BL) (BC), 40, 45 (TR), 51 (C)
Flintshire Record Office/Batsford, 4 (B)
Fotomas, 13 (TL), 15 (TL) (BL), 16 (R), 22 (B), 23 (TL), 32 (BR), 35 (T), 37 (TL) (B), 42, 43 (TR), 51 (BR), 53 (BR), 57 (TL), 61 (BR)
Greenwich Public Library, 33 (TL) (TR)
Guildhall Library/Sue Gooders, 11 (TR) (BL)
Sonia Halliday, 19 (BR), 35 (BR)
Tim Healey, 17 (T)
Mary Hillier Collection, 7 (BL)
K. Hoddle, 7 (BR)

Kodak Museum, 35 (BL)
Lady Lever Art Gallery, 27 (TR), 31 (BR)
Leighton House, 14
London Museum, 6 (BR), 38 (T), 39 (B), 50 (B)
London Transport Board/Batsford, 50 (T)
Mansell Collection, 9 (TR) (BL), 11 (BR), 13 (BL), 15 (TR), 16 (L), 29 (TL) (BL), 33 (TC) (BL), 52 (C) (R), 53 (L) (C), 56 (BL), 57 (TR)
George Morrison, 19 (BL)
Punch, 9 (BR)
By gracious permission of Her Majesty the Queen, 30
Radio Times Hulton Picture Library, 5 (B) (TL), 6 (B), 9 (TL), 12 (T), 13 (TR), 15 (BR), 20 (B), 21 (B), 22 (T), 23 (BR) (TR), 24-25, 28 (T) (B), 29 (R), 31 (BL), 34 (TL) (TR), 36 (L) (R), 37 (TR), 38 (B), 44 (T) (B), 45 (B), 46 (T), 49 (T) (C) (B), 51 (B) (BL), 57 (B), 60 (R)
R.I.B.A., 51 (T)
Science Museum, London, 56 (TL)
Sutcliffe Gallery/Batsford, 41 (BL)
Sir Benjamin Stone Collection/Batsford, 20-21, 41 (BR)
Tate Gallery, 11 (TL), 12 (B), 19 (T), 27 (TL), 31 (T)
Yorkshire Television, 3, 10

Artists
Ron Hayward Associates, (62-3)
Tony Payne 43 (TL), (55), (58-9)

Introduction

In 1851, Queen Victoria walked proudly among loyal crowds at the Great Exhibition where the marvels of Victorian invention were on show. In 1901, thousands of people came to mourn as her funeral procession passed through London. The 50 years between these two dates form the subject of this book. It was an exciting era.

By the end of the period, some city streets which had glowed with gas lamps now glittered with electric light. Stagecoaches had been replaced by steam engines, which were themselves being challenged by the first motor cars.

Working men had gained the right to vote, and governments were considering their needs. Children from working families could all go to school. Of course, there were still areas of appalling poverty, but dedicated people were urging reform.

Trade unions were demanding a larger share of the nation's wealth for working people. The poor could now buy frozen meat imported from Australia, and wear cheap, ready-made clothing. Many country-dwellers, tired of the small rewards of agriculture, had joined the thronging city populations, or emigrated to prospering colonies abroad. It was, on the whole, a time of peace, and most wars seemed distant skirmishes intended to make Great Britain greater.

These 50 years held a mixture of stability and change which laid the foundations for the way we live now. The new Yorkshire Television series *How We Used To Live* is set in a manufacturing town built between rugged Northern hills. The main character is a doctor who sees around him the good and bad effects of the industrial revolution. Episodes in his story illustrate the struggles and suffering, as well as the pleasures, of later Victorians.

The book may be used as background reading for the television series, or may be read independently as a stimulating introduction to this exciting period.

▲ Dr. Hughes' family entertaining guests, from Yorkshire Television's popular series *How We Used To Live,* covering the period 1874-87.

▼ Factory workers on their way to the mills (from the television series). The lives of the poor contrasted starkly with those of the rich.

Family Homes

It was convenient to build homes for working people in cramped rows, over-shadowed by the factories where they worked; they could walk to their jobs and start work early. But it was hardly pleasant. Few homes had gardens. Children played in cobbled alleys or backyards among rubbish and open drains. Outside water or earth closets were shared by neighbours. In most streets, water had to be fetched from a pump or standpipe.

Homes for the poor were not built with the needs of large families in mind. They merely provided 'one-up, one-down' or 'two-up, two-down' arrangements of rooms into which families had to fit as best they could. There was little privacy. It was stuffy when the small windows were closed for the winter. When they were open, the sooty air made it hard to keep clean.

In contrast, the lower middle classes often lived in rows of villas with small gardens at the back and front, and sometimes with the new luxuries of gas and water on tap.

Wealthier families often bought land and built houses to the west of a town, so the prevailing wind blew smoke and smells from poorer areas in the other direction. Architects designed elaborate houses to suit their individual requirements. These mansions had attics and basements, with perhaps a second staircase for the servants, and stables for the horses.

Every family home, whether rich or poor, had to be heated by coal, and much of a servant's day in a large house was spent tending fires. A middle class family might allow £12 a year of their budget for coal. With coal at 1/6 (7½p) a bushel, few working families could allow more than £4.

The rich spent about a tenth of their income on housing their families and servants. The poor paid low rents and dreaded eviction. They could be thrown ＿wing even a few shillings.

▲ Women spending washday outside, and enjoying the chance to gossip. They squeezed dirt from the clothes with their feet. Wet washing was dried and bleached in the sun. (For later developments, see page 34.)

▼ Working people shared communal water supplies at an outside pump. This one was at Holywell in Wales. The parish pump was a meeting place for the exchange of news and opinions.

◄ A Victorian middle-class family group. Three generations might live in one household. Six children was an average number

▼ A 'kitchener' was the centre of small family homes. The range had an oven for roasting and baking, and a hotplate for boiling.

Evening in the cottage; work goes on by the light of an oil lamp. Victorians loved to decorate their homes with pictures and ornaments. Even the poor collected trade calendars and pottery figures. Dusting took a long time.

A single room served as kitchen, living and dining room. The front of the coal-fired range had to be black-leaded every day to keep it looking smart.

A Wealthy Child's Life

Middle-class children were taught to 'know their place'. This was not in the parlour among breakable treasures and fine furniture. Victorians would have no childish tantrums or messy table-manners in the dining room. A child's place was in the nursery, upstairs with safety bars across the windows.

From birth, children might be looked after by a 'wet-nurse' so that their mother would not be disturbed by their needs. When children were about one month old, a Nanny was employed for about £25 a year to wash, dress and watch over them, amuse them, dose

them, take them out and teach them how to behave. Simple food was cooked in the nursery, or plain meals might be sent up from the kitchen.

If there were several children with a kindly Nanny and plenty of toys, life in the nursery was fun. For perhaps an hour a day, clean and tidy, the children were allowed downstairs to be with their parents. Some mothers taught the younger ones to read and write, and fathers sometimes taught their sons Latin.

As the children grew up, tutors and governesses were often employed, and they ranked halfway between servants and family. Boys were sometimes sent away to school, girls rarely.

Large homes were fun to explore, and children often made friends with the servants. In later life, they might well remember the groom who taught them to ride their first ponies, or the gardener who helped them make flower beds or vegetable patches.

But the richer the family, the more it was Nanny who ruled over the children. She would be remembered all their lives for twisting a little girl's ringlets into curling rags, putting a five-year-old boy into his first trousers (he wore frocks until then) and for her funny sayings, such as, 'We don't like that girl from Tooting Bec, she washes her face and forgets her neck.'

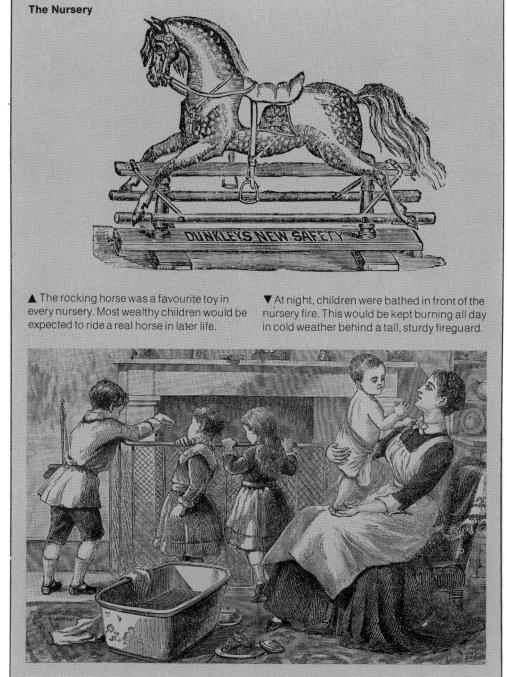

The Nursery

▲ The rocking horse was a favourite toy in every nursery. Most wealthy children would be expected to ride a real horse in later life.

▼ At night, children were bathed in front of the nursery fire. This would be kept burning all day in cold weather behind a tall, sturdy fireguard.

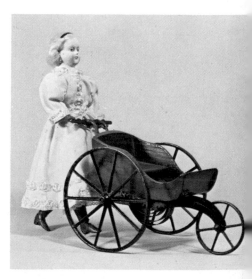

▲ Clockwork toys were popular. The mechanism was used mainly for train sets, but could be adapted for any toy. This is a clockwork Nanny, pushing a baby carriage.

Baby carriages were the forerunners of modern 'prams', which were designed later in the century. Prams allowed babies to lie down instead of being kept seated.

▲ Model theatres provided hours of amusement. Children could buy sheets of characters to cut out (penny plain; twopence coloured). There were books of play scripts adapted for the toy stage. Pollock's were the most famous.

◄ A Victorian fashion doll. These could be works of art. Lifelike heads were made from wax, porcelain, papier-mâché or the new material of celluloid. Bodies were of cloth or even kid.

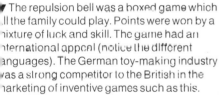

▼ The repulsion bell was a boxed game which all the family could play. Points were won by a mixture of luck and skill. The game had an international appeal (notice the different languages). The German toy-making industry was a strong competitor to the British in the marketing of inventive games such as this.

▲ These figures are strips from a zoetrope, one of many ingenious Victorian toys. The strips revolved inside a spinning drum. When glimpsed at speed, they appeared to be moving, much as cartoon figures do. Here a monkey, mounted on a dog, leaps a fence. A monster emerges from behind a closed door. A sweep emerges from a chimney to frighten a cat.

The tin drum was usually painted black, and rotated on a mahogany base. The figures were glimpsed through slits in the side (see project, page 63).

3. Too Young for the Mill

A Working Child's Life

▼ *The Dinner Hour, Wigan* a painting by Eyre Crowe. Girls and women could be as skilful and as quick as men at operating machines, but were paid half the wages.

Since 1844, women and young people had been restricted to a 12-hour working day. By 1878, there was a legal maximum of 60 hours a week.

The average wage was 10/- (50p) a week. From this, fines could be deducted for being late, for laughing or for sitting down. Women with families were often too tired to cook for the children or do housework after a day in a hot, damp, textile mill.

Of every ten babies born in factory towns like Salford, Birmingham and Sheffield, one would die before he was five (Registrar General's Report, 1891). A working mother might have to leave her baby with a 'minder' who drugged him to keep him quiet. Small children were often too weak from hunger to resist infection. Some who managed to survive on a poor diet became victims of tuberculosis or rickets. In spite of the resulting chest pains, fevers, or crooked backs and legs, these small wage-earners were made to work for their keep.

Gradually, during Victoria's reign, laws were passed to protect them. It became illegal to send boys under 12, or women and girls, down coal mines. In the 1870s, it also became illegal to employ 'half-timers' (children working 30 hours a week in factories, but also going to school) under the age of ten.

In the countryside, it was forbidden

(after 1876) for children under ten to work on the land, except at harvest time.

But the law was often ignored, and it was very difficult to control the amount of 'sweated labour' which children did at home. Part of the problem was that parents could not prevent more children being born than they could afford to feed and clothe. Each new baby might mean a brother or sister having to seek a job to help the family pay its way.

Fathers on low wages needed every penny their older children could earn. Employers used child labour because it was cheap.

Victorian reformers viewed this grim, tiring and unnatural childhood with increasing horror during the early years of the Industrial Revolution. Between 1842 and 1876, a series of laws was passed to protect children, and the worst miseries facing the working child had been considerably reduced.

◀ Children carrying clay in the brickyards, 1871. A girl of 12 was expected to handle 36 tons of bricks in one day.

▼ Laws prevented the employment of children in industry, but boys worked on the streets, sweeping crossings and shining shoes.

Street Arabs

'Hoo curls yer 'air, guv'nor?'

▲ Urchins in Britain's growing towns were known as 'street arabs'. They included runaway boys, too young to seek jobs and unwilling to go to school, who lived rough, sleeping in doorways and begging or stealing food.

◀ Working children and wandering street arabs enjoyed ice cream, a refreshing experience in the heat and dust. Halfpenny ices were sold from carts packed with ice to keep the contents chilled. They tasted like custard.

4. Never Too Late to Learn

Education

▼ The classroom of a Board School, a scene from the Yorkshire Television series *How We Used To Live.*

Parents could be taken to court and fined if their children were often absent without good reason. Magistrates occasionally sympathised if the family needed the child's earnings. Epidemics sometimes affected the attendance and a local excitement like a race meeting might cause large absentee figures. Children also played truant to avoid a caning, and many avoided lessons because they hated being taught with younger children who had reached the same standard.

Until 1870, it was a matter of chance whether or not poor children received an education. Churches and chapels had begun to set up Sunday Schools for working children on their only day off, so they could learn to read the Bible. These grew into weekday schools with more varied lessons. Huge classes of up to a hundred children were taught in a single room, seated in rows or standing in groups. One teacher was in charge, and older children, called 'monitors', were paid £6 a year to help. The pupils were expected to be clean, with their clothes mended.

For children who lived rough in the worst areas of cities there were 'ragged schools'. There were also places called 'dame schools', where a woman taught in her own home and where 20 children might be crammed into one small room. A few factory owners included schools for their workers' children in plans for model industrial villages.

But after 1870, education began to be available to all children aged between five and 13 years old. Local boards of governers were set up to build new schools if there were not enough in their area. The boards were also responsible for finding teachers to staff the new schools.

They were known as 'board schools'. The government gave sums of money, based on how many children came regularly and how well they progressed. Pupils were not put in classes according to their age. They were grouped in 'standards' according to how good they were at reading, writing and arithmetic.

Inspectors came once a year to test them. If a girl in Standard Two could do a long-division sum, she could go up to Standard Three, and the school was given a grant of 2/8d (about $13\frac{1}{2}$p) towards its costs. This 'Payment by Results' method restricted learning to dull repetition and a narrow range of subjects.

▲ The Regent Street Polytechnic. It was acquired in 1880 to house Quintin Hogg's Working Lads' Institute.

The adult education movement was growing with the help of the Drapers', Goldsmiths' and Clothworkers' companies. The City and Guilds Institute was founded in 1880 to promote evening classes and set technical examinations.

▲ *Kit's Writing Lesson* (1852) by R. B. Martineau. Many Victorians believed in self-help, and young men sometimes tried to learn at home.

Boys who aspired to office jobs needed good handwriting. First 'pothooks', then single letters, then words were practised. The aim was to develop the 'copperplate' style. In school, children in lower standards used slates and pencils. The young man above is struggling to control a pen, the nib full of ink, without making blots.

▲ Mill Hill Grammar School. Most schools for older boys were grammar schools. They were designed, like public schools, to prepare for the universities. Benefactors and religious groups often made gifts of money or land to support them. Latin was the main subject, but others like mathematics and natural science were gaining importance.

▲ Secondary education for girls was pioneered by Miss Buss and Miss Beale from the middle of the century onwards. It was thought unfeminine for young women to be 'blue-stockings' and try to ape their brothers. Wealthy parents were often slower than the poor to realise that well-educated daughters could be useful. Girls in the upper standards at board schools were taught how to be good wives and mothers. Here, girls are learning the value of the toothbrush; 'Spare the brush and spoil the TEETH!'

Medicine

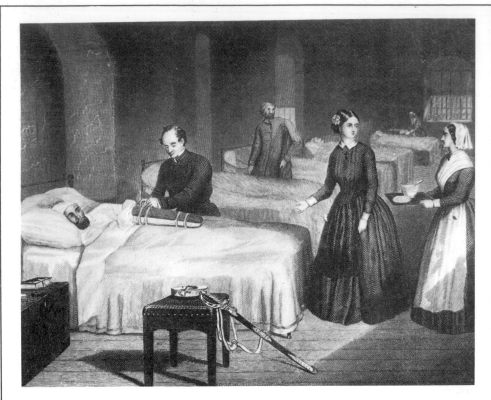

▲ Florence Nightingale in the hospital at Scutari during the Crimean War. In 1854, *The Times* revealed the sufferings of wounded British soldiers, comparing their dreadful conditions with the good treatment received by French soldiers.

Nurses in Britain tended to be ignorant gin-drinking old women. Miss Nightingale took a team of well meaning women to the Crimea; they learned their skills among patients who lay in agony on straw-filled sacks, pestered by vermin. After the war, Florence Nightingale returned to open a training school for nurses at St Thomas's Hospital in London.

Disease struck down both rich and poor in the 19th century. Vaccination had already been developed, and had reduced outbreaks of smallpox. Some attempts had been made to prevent epidemics by isolating patients with infectious diseases. But until 1875, there was no overall policy to deal with public health.

In 1875, however, a Public Health Act was passed. Local councils had to supply pure drinking water and to install covered drains and sewers. This helped to check the spread of water-borne diseases such as cholera. Councils had to remove rubbish and control offensive trades like leather tanning. This also helped to prevent ill-health. For too long, the homes of the poor had been surrounded by filth. Rich rate-payers had either to clean up areas, or risk falling ill themselves.

'Quack doctors' could still examine patients and prescribe pills and potions. But, unless on the Register of Qualified Doctors (1858), they were no longer allowed to sign death certificates.

There was no national health service, but many trained and dedicated doctors charged high fees to the rich so that they could treat the poor almost free of charge. There were also several free hospitals, set up by private charity, where doctors often treated patients for nothing.

Florence Nightingale transformed nursing – though she made a few enemies in the process. Elizabeth Garrett Anderson qualified as the first woman doctor, despite prejudice from many men. Two major discoveries made surgery less risky than ever before. Patients had suffered terribly on the operating table, and one in three had died because germs turned open wounds septic. Simpson introduced chloroform to relieve the pain, and Lister found that carbolic acid killed germs and disinfected surgical instruments. It was a time of great progress.

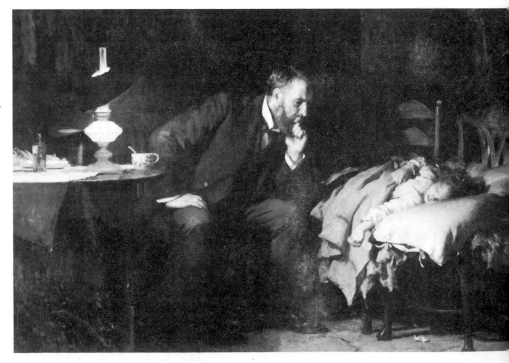

▲ *The Doctor*, a painting by Sir Luke Fildes. The Medical Act of 1858 led to the foundation of a General Medical Council to supervise the training of doctors, control examinations and maintain high standards in the profession. It did create a distinction between qualified and unqualified doctors, but did not forbid unqualified doctors to practise.

The
CARBOLIC SMOKE BALL
WILL POSITIVELY CURE
HAY FEVER.

A disease that has hitherto baffled the skill of the most eminent physicians who have sought in vain to cure or prevent its annual return.
WRITE FOR CIRCULAR AND TESTIMONIALS.
One **CARBOLIC SMOKE BALL** will last a family several summers, making it the cheapest remedy in the world at the price—10s. post free.
CARBOLIC SMOKE BALL CO.,
27, Princes-street, Hanover-square, London, W.

▲ Advertisements for patent medicines claimed amazing cures. A customer for one of these carbolic smoke balls took legal action when it failed to prevent influenza, and won £100 (1892).

Cheap remedies were sold on the street by unqualified doctors, or 'quacks'. A dose of patent medicine was often all the poor could afford, there was no free health service.

THE "SILENT HIGHWAY"-MAN.
"YOUR MONEY or your LIFE!"

Epidemics

◄ A dramatic cartoon by Tenniel (1858). It shows Death as 'The Silent Highwayman' on the noxious waters of the Thames.

Londoners drank from the filthy river, and other cities also suffered from polluted water supplies. Edwin Chadwick and John Simon were two reformers who argued fiercely for the cleansing of these 'poison beds' which did so much to create epidemics of disease.

Cholera claimed thousands of lives in 1867, after infected water reached a reservoir by accident. Smallpox, scarlet fever, diphtheria and typhoid attacked urban populations. It was a slow task proving to local authorites that better sanitation led to better health.

Even the Royal Family was not immune. The Prince Consort died of typhoid fever. The Prince of Wales was seriously ill in 1871, after staying at a house with bad drains.

Entertainment

As manufacturing towns grew and money flowed into them, there were new opportunities for entertainment. New playhouses and concert halls were built in industrial areas. The best performers in the world could be seen on provincial tours. People also entertained themselves, and after a dull day's work, the millworkers' brass band or the miners' choir would fill the evening with music.

Family entertainments were given at home. Guests were invited to 'high tea' or, in middle-class households, to dinner parties. They performed instrumental solos, parlour songs and recitations. Most Victorians tried to develop some talent to entertain. Tenors sang *Come into the Garden, Maud.* Elocutionists declaimed *The Boy Stood on the Burning Deck.*

Gilbert and Sullivan's popular operas began in 1875, and the Savoy Theatre was built specially for them. It was the first English public building to be lit by electricity.

Few great plays were written in the mid-19th century, but towards the end of the period, playwrights such as Shaw and Wilde were packing the theatres. Actors like Henry Irving were the superstars of the day, whilst the actresses Ellen Terry and Sarah Bernhardt compelled respect in an age when actresses were not generally thought respectable.

For the poor, there were peepshows, travelling fairs and circuses, a wide variety of street entertainers, seats in the gallery or the pit at the pantomine or the noisy revelry of the music halls.

To many people, the public house or 'pub' was a cheerful change from dismal homes and jobs. In rural areas the village inn was often the only place of entertainment, offering beer and skittles. Penny readings were held in church halls as rival attractions.

▼ *Conversation piece* (1884) by Joseph Solomon. After dinner, a party would go to the 'withdrawing' room. In this painting, the maid has spread a lace cloth and set a silver coffee service on the table. She adjusts an oil lamp so that the pianist can see the music. Photographs in an album and a silver frame are displayed.

Notice the bronze figures and the ornate plant stand (known as a *jardinière*) on the tiger-skin rug. The curtains and upholstery are luxurious.

▲ The palatial splendour of theatre design and construction made a Victorian night out into a special occasion. This advertisement is for the National Standard Theatre in London.

◀ An advertisement for *A Gaiety Girl* at the Prince of Wales' Theatre, 1894. This theatre specialised in lavish music hall entertainments.
Patriotic ballads formed the programmes of many early music hall shows. Later, comedy sketches and chorus girls were added. The audiences were mainly male. They ate and drank, arrived and left, whenever they chose.

▼ Ratting at the Blue Anchor Tavern in Finchley. Ratting was a cruel sport, but very popular in the middle of the 19th century. This picture shows Tiny, the 'wonder dog'.

▲ A building site provides the pitch for this street organ grinder. His costumed monkeys attract a crowd of fascinated children.

7. The Pledge
Temperance

The problem of drunkenness had grown with the city slums. In pubs and 'gin palaces', the poor found some escape from the miseries of their careworn lives. In many cases, the results were lost jobs, unpaid rent and hungry children. Wives were sometimes beaten if they dared to complain.

In 1830, taxes on beer and cider had been abolished. Anyone could open a beer shop for a fee of two guineas. In the singing and sprawling years that followed, the Temperance movement was founded. Its aims were to reform the drunkard, and educate the working class about the evils of strong drink.

Although there were wealthy men who were too fond of their wine, the main efforts of temperance workers were directed towards the poor, whose families suffered more when the breadwinner was too drunk to work.

Converts promised never to touch alcohol unless it was prescribed as medicine. Soon, even the doctor's prescription was ruled out. Those who completely abstained from alcohol were known as 'tee-totallers'.

The Band of Hope was formed for children, to spread the temperance message before they had got a taste for drink. There were thousands of members. Branch meetings were held in school and chapel halls up and down the country every week. Programmes included concerts, lectures, magic lantern shows and excursions. The audiences were introduced to sweet, fizzy drinks as non-alcoholic alternatives to beer. (Beer was safer than foul water and cheaper than tea at first.)

In 1853, Gladstone delighted temperance workers by cutting the tax on tea imports. Tea became the everyday drink of the nation. Temperance reformers never managed to have alcohol banned completely, but they did manage to have the sale of alcohol controlled. The ultimate outcome was a strange set of licensing laws.

▲ Drinking outside a pub in 1875. Beer was a treat which even the poorest could afford. At this time, the nation consumed 34 gallons of beer per head every year. The price was fairly constant. A pint cost between 2d and 3d (about 1p).

▶ Lyrics of two Temperance songs. Audiences would be expected to shed tears over the fate of the drunkard's child, and to join in the chorus in praise of cocoa.
  The picture above shows illustrations from a Temperance Pledge leaflet called *A Looking Glass For Drunkards* which warned of the drunkard's fate.

A LOOKING GLASS FOR DRUNKARDS
DRUNKENNESS LEADS TO
Murders, Rapes, Fires, Shipwrecks, Sabbath Breaking, Blasphemy, Seditions, Gambling, Fighting, Loss of Employment, Loss of Character, Beggary, Ignominy, & the Gallows.

Father's a Drunkard
*"Out in the gloomy night, sadly I roam,
I have no mother dear, no pleasant home,
Nobody cares for me, no-one would cry
Even if poor little Bessie should die.
Barefoot and tired I've wandered all day
Asking for work; but I'm too small, they say.
On the damp ground I must now lay my head,
Father's a drunkard and mother is dead.*

Cocoa
Chorus:
*"'Tis cocoa, cocoa, a steaming cup of cocoa;
'Twill warm your hands and cheer your hearts
I tell you what I think:
Like cocoa, cocoa, we ought to make life's
                                    yoke, oh,
As pleasant, bright and good for all as this
                                    delicious drink!"*

◀ Signing the pledge, an illustration of 1887. To help a reformed drunkard to keep his promise to abstain from alcohol, he was given a card. His new and solemn undertaking was printed upon it. He had to sign the card, and keep it by him as a constant reminder. In some homes, the pledge cards were framed and proudly displayed. Other cards, brought home by children who had taken the pledge without permission, were torn up by angry parents.

▼ A Temperance rally at the Crystal Palace in 1872. The audience was entertained by a Band of Hope choir of 6,000 voices.

Rallies were held to demonstrate the strength of the movement, so that changes in public opinion about drink might follow. Temperance orators challenged the Government to prohibit the sale of alcohol, and mocked the House of Lords as an assembly of the 'Beerage'.

The Farm Labourer

Until about 1850, most people had lived in the country. But by the middle of the 19th century as many people lived in towns. From then on, the urban population surpassed that of the countryside.

In the heart of the countryside, wages could be as low as 6/- (30p) a week. Many farm workers moved to towns, or emigrated. Closer to the towns, where the better-paid factory jobs beckoned, farmers had to pay their labourers higher wages to persuade them to stay on the land.

A man called Joseph Arch formed a trade union for farm workers, and during the 1870s their conditions improved as a result. But then came a series of ruined harvests and epidemics of disease among livestock.

British farming suffered further as cheap food began to flood in from abroad. Steamships brought vast quantities of wheat from the American prairies, where the growth of railways and the use of agricultural machinery ha[d] boosted production. The developmen[t] of refrigeration meant that frozen mea[t] could now be shipped to Britain fro[m] Australia. (Previously, sheep had bee[n] reared in Australia mainly for thei[r] wool, and much of the meat was le[ft] surplus.) British dairy farmers als[o] suffered when margarine was intro[-]duced as a cheap substitute for butte[r].

The countryside declined, and man[y] landowners faced ruin. In the rura[l] hamlets, labourers faced a bleak futur[e] in their decaying 'tied cottages'. Road[s] fell into disrepair and communitie[s] were isolated. The carrier's cart was th[e] only regular link with the nearest marke[t] town. Winter was dark and depress[-]ing, and children had to walk man[y] miles to school. Yet they had one grea[t] advantage over poor children in towns[:] the air was clean and fresh. A fine summe[r] and a good harvest in surroundings o[f] peace and beauty was better than slu[m] life.

▼ *Answering the Emigrant's Letter* (1850), by James Collinson. The picture shows a slightly idealised interior of a farm-worker's home, for this was a time when thousands of countrymen left the miseries of rural life in Britain to seek new lives abroad.

The news from abroad may have described gold strikes in California or sheep shearing in Australia, settling in New Zealand with Maori neighbours or the grandeur of the Canadian forests. The reply may have described the family's own intention of going abroad. In a single year (1852), 32,700 emigrants left Britain.

▲ A Cottage at Hambledon by Birket Foster. Thatched roofs and crumbling walls may have looked picturesque, but they were damp and unhealthy, especially in winter. Victorian architects began to experiment with new designs for labourer's cottages (see pages 54-55).

▲ A family evicted from their home in Ireland where rural conditions were worse than anywhere else in Britain.

The failure of potato harvests caused widespread famine. The land was owned by English landlords who came to be regarded as foreign oppressors. Rents were impossibly high, and even when crops failed they had to be paid. Unpaid rent meant being evicted (thrown out).

Whole families wandered off across the fields to starve, and their homes were destroyed to prevent them coming back. The British Government's failure to act to protect poor tenants against their landlords was blamed for constant unrest in Ireland. Violence erupted and demands for self government were made.

Meanwhile, a million people emigrated to Canada and the United States, whilst 600,000 went to England. Ireland lost about a third of her population through famine and emigration.

▲ The Victorian steam plough Noreen on display at a fair near Oxford in 1972.

Steam ploughs could be hired by the day, but were used only on the biggest farms. Workers feared that mechanised farming would threaten their own livelihood. A traction engine did the work of 30 horses.

Elections

In 1848, an enormous petition was presented to Parliament. It was the last effort of the Chartist movement to gain for every householder the right to vote. The petition, said to contain five million names, proved to be something of a joke. The forged signatures of the Queen and the Duke of Wellington appeared on it again and again. The petition brought ridicule on the movement, yet in the next half-century almost all its demands were to be met.

The Reform Act of 1867 gave the vote to men in towns. There had been a steady increase in national wealth. Trade unions and Co-operatives were growing. Industrial workers were gaining strength. In spite of setbacks, and ministers resigning in protest, Disraeli managed to push his Reform Bill through Parliament. From now on, male householders paying the poor rate, and male lodgers, would be entitled to take part in electing governments.

Employers, landlords or union leaders might try to coax or bully them into supporting a favoured candidate. But after 1872, every voter could make his choice in secret.

Almost all townsmen could now vote. Yet agricultural workers had no such right until 1884. Then Gladstone gave the counties, mainly large farming areas, the same qualifications for voting as those which applied in towns. This brought the number of British electors to five million, including the great majority of adult males.

Women were excluded from voting until well into the 20th century. It was not surprising, since universities had opened their doors to women, that there was growing agitation from women for the right to vote. The movement was led, from the 1870s, by Rhoda Garrett. But her meetings did not arouse widespread concern, and resolutions put before Parliament died a quiet death. Most Victorian women were not interested.

TO THE

ELECTORS

OF THE

BOROUGH OF STAMFORD.

GENTLEMEN,

Having now completed my Canvass, I take the earliest opportunity of announcing to my friends that the result has been most satisfactory; I therefore request that you will accept my best thanks for the kind and gratifying manner in which I have been received.

As the Election is fixed for Monday next at 10 o'clock precisely, I earnestly request the attendance of my Friends at the George Hotel, Saint Martin's, on that morning, at Half-past 9 o'clock, to accompany me from thence to the Hustings.

I have the honor to be, Gentlemen,

Your obliged and faithful Servant,

ROBERT G. CECIL.

▲ In 1853, all the electors were 'Gentlemen'!

◀ An election meeting in East Birmingham in 1892. By this time, every male householder in Britain could take part in elections. A few women have joined the crowd listening to the speeches; they may have held opinions, but they had no right to vote. In the 1892 election the first Labour candidate was elected. His name was Keir Hardie, and he formed the Independent Labour Party one year later.

▲ Bill posting in 1880. Elections could be rowdy. Opponents heckled each other's meetings and threw missiles. In this sketch, rivals cover up each other's posters.

▼ At last, in the General Election of 1880, '£30,000 a year and 30/- a week' have equal rights in the secret ballot. Four years after this, farm labourers could also vote.

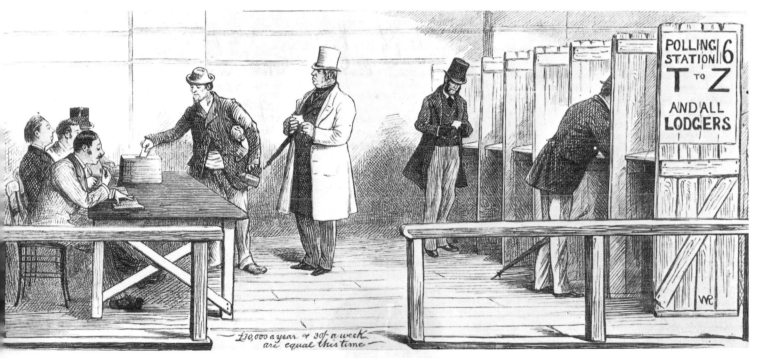

The Festive Season

Queen Victoria's husband, Prince Albert is thought to have brought the first Christmas tree to Britain, for the delight of the Royal Family. But there was already an array of festive Christmas customs in Britain, some dating back to pagan times.

The Yule Log was a feature of the country Christmas. It smouldered throughout the holiday, which came to an end when the log burnt out. The charred embers were saved to kindle the fire the following Christmas. Holly and mistletoe were hung indoors, but it was thought unlucky for women to carry them in.

It was a season of giving, encouraged by Charles Dickens in his book *A Christmas Carol*. The gentry gave blankets and coal and plum pudding to their estate workers. Domestic servants were given presents and a holiday on Boxing Day. Carol-singers and bell-ringers were given coppers at the doors of middle-class homes.

'Wassaillers' carried boughs and cribs of ribbon and evergreen through town or village, 'mummers' performed old, traditional plays based on St. George and the Dragon, and all were rewarded.

On farms, a special sheaf of wheat was hung from the rafters at harvest-time to make the Christmas 'frumenty', a hot, thick, white, spicy drink. Extra feeds were taken out to the farm animals, and a sheaf of corn was nailed to the barn roof for the birds.

For children, there were stockings filled with fruit and nuts, and Christmas puddings containing silver coins and charms. There were spooky games like Snapdragon, when someone, dressed in a white sheet, carried into a darkened room a bowl of raisins in burning brandy. The game was to risk the weird blue flames and snatch the raisins without getting scorched fingers.

When Christmas was over, town children could look forward to a trip to the annual pantomime.

▲ Prince Albert introduces the Royal Family to the first Christmas tree, 1848.

▼ Father Christmas with a sackful of presents, as depicted on a Victorian Christmas card.

▲ Christmas waits (carol singers). They developed from the waits of the past; official bands of musicians maintained by cities and towns.

▲ Mr Pickwick on the ice. Dickens' books were favourite reading for all the family, and he did as much as anybody to popularise the idea of the festive season among Victorians.

– A Victorian Christmas party for children of wealthy families. Christmas crackers were known as 'bon-bons'.

▲ 'Deep and crisp and even'; snowfall on a Victorian street.

▼ Harvesting in 1893. The whole of a country village might help out. Travelling workers sometimes hired themselves out for wheat and barley harvests, moving from south to north for the early and later ripenings.

The Role of the Church

At least half the population went to church on Sundays, all worshipping God according to their different practices. Roman Catholics went to Mass, and there were Church of England services in every parish. There were Christians known as 'non-conformists' who belonged to smaller groups, Methodists, Baptists and Congregationalists, for example. They built their chapels wherever there was enough local support. Quakers went to meeting houses to worship, whilst Salvationists went to 'citadels'.

The different groups did not always get on well with one another, and there was some hypocrisy. But there was also plenty of Christian charity. Dedicated Christians of every sort inspired reform and gave practical help to the needy.

In 1859, Charles Darwin published his *Origin of Species*, which suggested that humans had evolved very gradually from earlier forms of life. This caused a sensation, for it cast doubt on the Biblical account of Adam and Eve. Debates about Darwinism were fierce.

Every responsible citizen was expected to profess belief in God. A Northampton M.P. was excluded from Parliament for refusing to take the oath, as he was an atheist.

Laws were passed to make Sunday a day of rest. This was called 'Sabbath Observance'. Only work which was 'of necessity or charity' was permitted. One barber's apprentice refused to shave customers on Sunday, and the House of Lords upheld his case against his master.

Toys were put away on Sunday. Books were only allowed if they were of a moral and improving nature. Families walked to Church in Sunday clothes and servants were supposed to attend as well. There was little else to do anyway. Public sports and amusements were forbidden, and all shops were closed.

◄ A Victorian christening, painted by James Charles. Church ceremonies played an important part in people's life, from birth to death.

► A Victorian undertaker with his hearse. Even the poor valued a proper funeral. A pauper burial was the final shame.

◄ *The Village Choir* (1847) by Thomas Webster. A fine singing voice was a source of great pride, and a good choir was considered a great benefit to the community.

▼ A Victorian bride prepares for her wedding. A woman's role was that of wife and mother. Divorce courts were established in 1857, but marriages seldom ended in divorce. The poor could not afford the cost, and the rich preferred to avoid the scandal.

12. On the Parish
Poverty and Relief

The Government was supposed to care for the hungry and the homeless. In every district, a Poor Law Union had a duty to feed and shelter them. But there was the belief that no pauper should be fed or housed more generously than the poorest wage-earner; and some wages were very low indeed.

People who were forced to ask for help were herded into grim, gloomy workhouses. Here, husbands and wives, parents and children were separated. They slept in draughty dormitories and spent their days in tough or tedious work. Meals were dull, and only sufficient to keep them alive.

Nobody risked going to the workhouse if they could possibly survive by any other means. This left the orphans, the sick and the aged. They made up the bulk of the workhouse population, and there was no point in making their lives a misery to deter them from seeking help; they had no choice.

Workhouse Visiting Societies urged reform, and conditions did improve gradually. But one aspect of the law was generally ignored. This was the requirement to provide married quarters for elderly couples. It was seldom fulfilled. Aged husbands and wives, who might have spent a lifetime together, were separated and spent their last years apart.

Destitute children were able to attend local Board Schools after 1870. It was easy to see which members of a class came from the Workhouse. Girls had their hair cropped, and boys' heads were shaved close to the skull. They wore drab uniforms and grew up shamed by their poverty.

Luckily, there were private charities which provided alternative aid. Soup kitchens, night refuges and children's homes were run on voluntary contributions. But these were random efforts to cope with a problem only Parliament could solve.

▲ Dinner time in St Pancras' Workhouse in about 1900. This picture was supposed to show improvements in conditions, but notice that husbands were still separated from wives.

▼ Voluntary contributions financed this night refuge for those who found it too cold to sleep out. A middle-class benefactor reads aloud from the Bible. The illustration is by Gustave Doré.

◄ A destitute woman minding a child in 1875. Even a cold doorstep may have seemed friendlier than the Workhouse.

▲ Listlessness and depression in an East End slum. The poor paid up to half their incomes in rent for miserable quarters like these.

◄ The poor could not afford new possessions. Most bought clothes and furniture from second hand shops, pawning them in times of hardship. Some clothes were sixth or seventh hand.

Holidays and Leisure

The idea of leisure for working people grew up gradually during the 19th century. Time was allowed off for feast days linked to events in the church calendar. Hours of work for men in factories were cut, largely because of the exhausting effect these same hours had on women and children. There was a growing interest in Saturday afternoon sport among the working class.

Cricket and football, boxing and wrestling attracted spectators. Race meetings were popular among all classes. For the middle class, the range of leisure activities was wider, and included genteel sports for ladies. Despite their long skirts, girls could go boating, play tennis and croquet, beat their brothers at archery and ride side-saddle.

The idea of holidays began to emerge. The rich sent sons for educational tours of Europe, and daughters on social visits to enlarge their acquaintance with marriageable men.

The seaside was at first a fashionable playground for the rich. The middle classes soon followed. Doctors sent patients for cures at spas where the water was supposed to have medicinal properties. They also stressed the virtues of sea air and sea bathing. Children were taken on holiday to improve their health.

Most families who could afford it began to spend a few weeks away from home every summer. Workers had no chance to leave their jobs for as long as this. But in 1871, Bank Holidays were introduced in England and Wales.

For workers, it was a whole day off and it wasn't even a Sunday! Railways brought the seaside within reach of all but the poorest. Crowds rushed to new resorts on special excursion trains. Wagonettes carried picnickers to the countryside. The poor of London steamed down the Thames or flocked to Hampstead Heath.

▼ *Ramsgate Sands* (1851-3) by William Powell Frith. Frith was a Victorian artist who specialised in portraying crowds at leisure. Another example of his work can be seen on the facing page.

'It is difficult to walk through the throng,' said *The Observer* in 1865, 'The portion of the beach allotted to the men is crowded with well-dressed females, who look on without a blush or a giggle.' Sea breezes blew away maidenly modesty.

Frith's *Derby Day* was first shown in 1858. Epsom race-course attracted both rich and poor, from royalty down to vagabonds and pickpockets. The races were not the only entertainment. Acrobats, strong men and escapologists performed to entertain the crowds.

Ragged children could gape at the fashionable rich, and countrymen in smocks could mingle with gentlemen in top hats and frock coats.

The most exciting Derby was in 1896, when the Prince of Wales' horse Persimmon won. It was a sign of the Prince's popularity that the Epsom crowd from every walk of life cheered him spontaneously to the echo. (For a third crowd scene by Frith see page 51).

▲ Serious-looking holiday-makers take a donkey ride at Whitby Bay sands.

◀ Bank holiday, 1892. It was still rather daring to show an ankle. Bathing dresses were voluminous. Women had to change in the privacy of a bathing machine, which was pulled into the sea by horses. If this was too expensive, a discreet paddle cost nothing.

▲ Boating at Boulter's Lock. Sailing and rowing on Britain's inland waters were more tranquil and elegant pastimes than bustling around on the beach. The number and variety of small pleasure craft developed considerably during the 19th century.

Working People

In the Victorian Age, people were expected to look after themselves and not rely on others to help them. This was known as 'self-help'. If a man's wage fell below the cost of his needs, he had to do without them.

In order to be sure of fair wages and conditions, working men began to join together to make trade unions. The first Trade Union Congress (T.U.C.) was formed in 1868, and between 1871 and 1875, men in major industries gained legal rights for their unions.

They could now vote and strike. Regular meetings of the T.U.C. provided occasions for strengthening bonds between the different unions.

Years of settled prosperity allowed 'real' wages to rise. Although wages did drop from time to time, prices tended to fall with them, so the effects were not disastrous. Over-all, factory workers in regular employment could now afford a higher standard of living.

Many hand-skilled workers suffered, however. Much of their trade had been taken over by machines. For example, handloom weavers who had once been highly paid were reduced to poverty.

Amongst the worst-paid were 'out-workers' at sweated trades, such as hand-finishing garments or making matchboxes. They had to work hard at low rates, and it was impossible for their earnings to keep up with prices; there were not enough hours in the day. They had no trade unions, and many were widows or single women struggling against starvation. Women were paid less than men, for it was not accepted that they might be family breadwinners.

At the turn of the century, two men, Rowntree in York and Booth in London, did surveys on workers' conditions. These shattered the belief that all working people were prospering. They proved that a 'submerged tenth' of the population, about three million people, lived in hopeless destitution.

▲ Sweatshop dressmakers suffered long working days for as little as 4/- (20p) a week.

▼ Men in this Dartford engineering works had 35/- (£1.75p) a week for their skills.

▼ A bricklayer's trade union card. Men in the building industry could earn 35/- too.

Chimney sweeps had guaranteed employment, for every household burned coal. A man and boy together could earn 6/- (30p) a day, and more in winter and spring. Some sweeps, like the one shown above, used brushes on long rods instead of climbing-boys, even when old-fashioned customers objected.

▲ Covent Garden porters. Unskilled casual labour was rewarded by about 5d (2p) an hour. At two o'clock in the morning, the first fruit and vegetables began to arrive at the market. There were ranks among the market vendors. Proud costermongers with their own barrows looked down on hawkers with trays.

▲ A rabbit-seller walks the street. It was reckoned in 1881 that 1.87 pennyworth (less than 1p) of meat was eaten per head per day. Middle class families ate vast quantities of meat, but the poor had next to none. A rabbit bought from a street vendor like this would vary the monotonous diet.

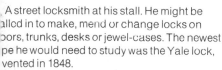

A street locksmith at his stall. He might be called in to make, mend or change locks on doors, trunks, desks or jewel-cases. The newest type he would need to study was the Yale lock, invented in 1848.

Notice the stout leather apron and the variety of tools.

▲ Miners in their occupational dress. These two men were rescuers at a pit disaster. From 1850, all fatal accidents in coal mines had to be reported. In 1851, 984 deaths were recorded. A National Miners' Association was formed in 1856, and this, with a recognition of the dangers and necessities of the job, brought wages up to 25/8d.

▲ A ginger cake seller in 1884. Income from passers-by was unreliable and seldom amounted to a living wage. Street vendors' cries, calling attention to their wares, made a walk through town exciting to middle-class children. Poor children earned a few coppers by sweeping crossings or selling flowers.

Inventions and Daily Life

The 19th century was an age of invention. No sooner had Victorians come to take for granted the powers of steam and gas than they were faced with the wonders of electricity.

In 1882, an Electrical Exhibition was held at the Crystal Palace. An electric lighting section pointed the way to future changes in the home. Already, three London railway stations and the streets of Liverpool, Bristol and Brighton were lit by electricity. At the Crystal Palace, a miniature electric railway was on display.

By the end of the century, passengers boarded electric trams and trains without fear, and were ready to ride under ground on the 'Tuppeny Tube'.

There were steam powered vehicles on the roads. An Act of 1865 limited their speed to 4 mph (about 6 kph). man carrying a red flag had to walk ahead to warn other road-users. 'Horseless carriages' like the *Milord* steam phaeton and the petroleum gig of 1895 were also subject to this law until it was removed in 1896. On the whole, however, Britain lagged behind other countries in developing motor cars.

There were other surprises for later Victorians. Telephones, bicycles, submarines, refrigerators, steel ships, typewriters, gramophones and cinemas were topics of astonished conversation. Even the poor marvelled at them, though they did not expect any direct benefit.

Cheap travel did influence their lives however, and there were several other changes. Sewing-machines, adapted to mass-produced clothing or boot and shoe-making, cut the cost of being respectably dressed. Telephone exchanges provided good jobs for women. New machines were invented for composing printers' type. These brought down the cost of newspapers, just as a whole generation of working people was learning to read. And lucky children could learn to write with another invention: the fountain pen!

▲ A gas stove of 1873. Gas companies began to hire out their cookers in the 1870s to let people see how they liked them.

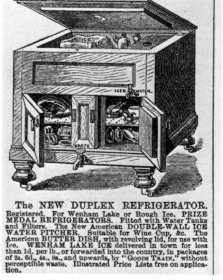

The NEW DUPLEX REFRIGERATOR.
Registered. For Wenham Lake or Rough Ice. PRIZE MEDAL REFRIGERATORS. Fitted with Water Tanks and Filters. The New American DOUBLE-WALL ICE WATER PITCHER. Suitable for Wine Cup, &c. The American BUTTER DISH, with revolving lid, for use with Ice. WENHAM LAKE ICE delivered in town for less than 1d. per lb., or forwarded into the country, in packages of 2s. 6d., 4s., 8s., and upwards, by "GOODS TRAIN," without perceptible waste. Illustrated Price Lists free on application.

▲ Food could be chilled in lead-lined cabinets with drainage holes. This one has a tap for iced drinking water.

▼ Mincing machines were called 'choppers' at first. They appeared in the 1880s.

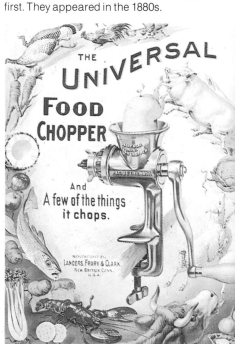

▲ Early sewing machines were ugly, but for the home needlewoman they were produced as decorative furniture.

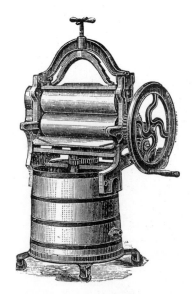

▲ Much of the fatigue of washday was relieved by the invention of combined washing and mangling machines.

▲ Visitors at the Paris Exhibition of 1889 listening to the phonograph. It used a mouthpiece stylus, pressing on a tinfoil plate revolving on a drum, to scratch the sound vibrations of the human voice. These could then be played back through tubes to earpieces. By 1900, the clockwork gramophone had arrived, playing vulcanite discs through a horn.

▲ A Victorian steam road roller on display at a fair near Oxford, 1972. These machines were used to give new roads a level surface.

◄ A bellows camera of the 1880s. In 1884 emulsion-coated celluloid was produced, and in 1888, roll-film cameras appeared. Family snapshots were now easy to take.

Law and Order

In the mid-19th century, Britain's new police forces were trying to prevent crime. But little was done to reform convicted criminals. In past generations, many had been hanged for minor misdeeds, or sent to the colonies. After 1852, Tasmania refused to accept any more convicts. Transportation to penal settlements ended in 1867.

That same year, London police estimated that 100,000 of the city's population lived on the proceeds of crime. Each main town had its underworld. The hundreds of cells in vast new prison buildings throughout the nation were filled to capacity.

In 1877, these prisons became th responsibility of the Home Secretar (in the past, they had been supporte by local rates and controlled b magistrates).

Two theories about prison life wer being applied at this time. The 'separ ate' system meant solitary confinemen the prisoner eating and working alon in his cell all the time. The 'silen system allowed convicts to eat and wor together but never to speak. At exercis in Pentonville, convicts wore caps wit masks so they could not even recognis one another.

Brutal punishment was declining, governors found they could keep orde by granting and taking away privilege rather than flogging. Tedious hours the treadwheel, or oakum picking, th crank, or at shot-drill (passing iron bal weighing 24 lbs along a line and bac again) were enough to deter a pett thief from risking a second prison term Between 1851 and 1891, the rate imprisonment per head of the popu lation fell by three-quarters.

The main reason for improved la and order was the growth of profession police forces. There were still 22 countie managing with amateurs in 1853. Th Police Act of 1856 made all countie keep a paid constabulary.

◀ An old fashioned 'Peeler' of 1860, with juvenile delinquents. A boy of 11 would serve 18 months in prison for robbing a shop-till in 1850, and 7 day for sleeping out.

▼ A police patrol in Whitechapel in the 1870s. Notice the new uniform. Regular patrols revealed criminals, but they also allowed police to report o conditions of poverty where vice flourished.

'JACK THE RIPPER'S ATTEMPT TO MURDER 'ONE-ARMED LIZ'

A FRIEND OF ONE OF HIS MANY VICTIMS

The Victorians were fascinated by crime, and Conan Doyle's Sherlock Holmes stories became immensely popular. This picture shows an episode from one real life case; that of Jack the Ripper in 1888.

Female convicts at work during the silent hour in Brixton prison. Elizabeth Fry, who died in 1845, had reformed conditions for women prisoners beyond recognition. Their uniform was respectable, their work useful.

The prisoners in the numbered cubicles are working the treadmill. Those in the foreground are picking oakum. The work is carried out under the silent system, and the men change places every 15 minutes.

Civic Pride

During the second half of the 19th century, both Parliament and local officials concerned themselves increasingly with the quality of life in towns.

Town halls resounded with speeches from mayors, aldermen and councillors on how ratepayers' money might best be spent. Public-spirited men often had great private interest in their areas. Party politics became bogged down in such weighty problems as where to site a sewage farm, who should build the library, or how to cure a smoke nuisance.

If the men who governed a town were also its main employers and owned much of the property, the town's health and prosperity became their chief concern. Men who had made fortunes in industry left them to the town for purposes dear to their hearts. Hospitals, colleges, parks and art galleries would perpetuate their names, and marble statues recall their images.

The ugly sprawl of factories and workers' dwellings was often hidden behind corporation offices, free trade halls, municipal theatres and Mechanics Institutes, all of architectural magnificence.

Other concerns extended the great panorama. Banks, railway stations, chapels and churches thrust noble domes, spires and turrets into the sooty clouds. These buildings were symbols that the dirty town was rich, and that its inhabitants deserved the best.

Often there was keen rivalry between one town and the next. It would not be thought a waste of money to surround a drinking fountain with statues, or to perch a decorative Gothic clock tower on a tram shed.

Towards the end of the century, councils concentrated more on their services, with gas and water works, electricity supplies, police forces and fire brigades. More money also went on roads, housing and education.

▲ *Pentonville Road and St Pancras* by John O'Connor. Notice the horse-drawn omnibuses in the street.

St Pancras station was built in the 'Gothic' style, with spires and buttresses imitating the cathedrals of the Middle Ages. This grand style was much admired by the Victorians, and applied to all sorts of unlikely buildings.

▲ An elephant ride at the London zoo, 1900. Animals had once been kept at the Tower of London, but in 1829 they were taken over by the Royal Zoological Society, and transferred to Regent's Park. Municipal zoos were set up in many other cities. The one in Dublin became famous for its lions; more than 100 were born there during the 19th century.

▼ Lighting a gas street lamp. By 1870, there were 49 municipal gasworks in England and Wales. Councils borrowed heavily, but eventual profits from the works paid for other schemes.

◀ A Clydebank fire brigade of 1896. Notice the steam pump engine. It was drawn by horses and the steam power was used to ensure a steady jet of water on the flames. This was a great improvement on earlier hand-pumped engines which only produced irregular squirts.

▼ Hyde Park in London. The growth of towns made parks increasingly valuable for health and recreation.

Village Life

▼ The village street, Greystone Bird. Despite low wages, country dwellers led lives in many ways more satisfactory than those of town dwellers. There were no civic amenities, but the pace of life was slower, the air was pure and people were among trees and fields.

Oil lamps or candles shining from windows lit the streets at night. Most families had their own closet in the garden. Water was carried from the communal pump. There was a country calendar of events to enjoy; Maypole dancing, haymaking, apple-picking and the hunt.

In towns, it was possible for ambitious businessmen to rise high in society. But in country districts, the landed gentry still headed the social order as they had done for centuries. They formed what was known as the 'squirearchy'.

The lord of the manor, his eldest son, and neighbouring wealthy families were at the top. A little below came the village parson.

Next came those with special skills needed in village life; the blacksmith, the wheelwright who mended wagons, the carpenter who built barns. There was the miller, the saddler, the shoemaker and, more recently, the village schoolmaster. All were on a level with farmers and estate bailiffs, smallholders, carriers and shopkeepers.

Farmworkers such as shepherds, who looked after animals, were considered superior to the labourers who dug ditches, hoed turnips or spread manure.

Some work was done by casual labour; harvesting, sheep-shearing or hedge-cutting, for example. Regular employees had greater security. They would be hired in November, and move in with their families to cottages which went with their jobs. Wives might be employed in the dairy, and there was always plenty of work for children to do. Weeding, stone-picking and bird scaring were common tasks.

Wages varied from region to region. In 1851, a Lancashire labourer received 15/- (75p) a week compared to the 6/- (30p) paid in Wiltshire. Part of the wage was sometimes paid in beer or cider until 1887, when the Truck Act was passed. This demanded that payment should be made entirely in cash.

Membership of Joseph Arch's agricultural trade union slumped during the late 1870s when poor harvests bankrupted some farmers. But it rose again briefly when farmworkers were given the right to vote in 1884. In 1885, Arch became the first agricultural labourer to win a seat in Parliament.

▲ A team of oxen on a farm in Kent in about 1800. The 'stockman', who looked after the animals, held a higher position than the ordinary farm worker. Beasts and men still did much of the farm work. In the 1870s, for example, only a quarter of grain harvesting was done by machine.

▲ Farm workers with yokes and milk churns. During the second half of the 19th century, more improvements in productivity came through better tools than through new machinery.

◀ Market day at Whitby. The isolation of village life was eased by weekly journeys to the nearest market town. Those who could not go to sell their own produce sent it by carrier's cart. The carrier was an important link between town and country.

Progress

▼ The early Victorian era was a time of exhibitions. The Great Exhibition of 1851 was a huge display of British designs and inventions held in the Crystal Palace, a huge structure of iron and glass.

Daily attendance often exceeded 60,000. On four days a week, entry cost only 1/- (5p). Humble families from all over the country arrived by train for this rare treat. There were sections for raw materials, for manufacturing, for science and the fine arts. Refreshments consumed by visitors included 113 tons of meat and 1,046 gallons of pickles.

The exhibitions were aimed at encouraging further development and competition between manufacturers. The fountain at the 1862 Exhibition is illustrated here.

By the turn of the century, the older Victorians could look back on five decades of progress. Much of this was due to invention and discovery. Novelties at the time of the Great Exhibition had now become commonplace and stimulated more new ideas. The mid-century invention of the telegraph, for example, was followed by the telephone of the 1870s, wireless telegraphy in the 1890s, and Marconi's radio signals from Cornwall to Newfoundland in 1901.

Science fiction writers began to imagine the 20th century. Jules Verne published *Twenty Thousand Leagues Under The Sea* (1869) and *Around the World in Eighty Days* (1873). H. G. Wells offered *The Time Machine* (1895) *The War of the Worlds* (1898) and *The First Men in the Moon* (1901). Wells had been influenced by Darwin's theory of evolution and argued that if humans had evolved (developed gradually) from lower animals, might not society be improving itself in the same way? In a book called *Anticipations* (1901) Wells suggested that society was evolving towards a utopia.

There were many reasons why Victorians might feel confident about the future. In 1845, Disraeli had written a novel called *Sybil*, in which he described Britain as being a land of 'two nations'; rich and poor. Now the middle class was drawing into its growing numbers more prosperous artisans, traders and skilled workers, clerks and young people from poor backgrounds educated for the professions. The gap between rich and poor was narrowing. Samuel Smiles' doctrine of *Self-help*, published in 1859, was accepted by many Victorians as the recipe for success in life.

Areas of shameful poverty did still exist, but they were being exposed, and now shocked the Victorian conscience. It was no longer accepted that such things were natural.

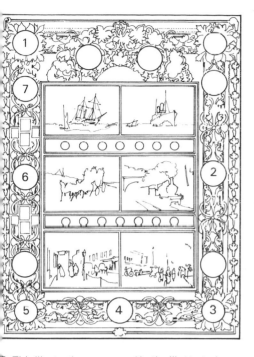

▶ This illustration appeared in *the Illustrated London News* of 1897 to show the enormous progress that had been made in the 60 years since Queen Victoria had come to the throne. Around the central pictures are some of Britain's greatest scientists and inventors.

1 Charles Darwin, whose *Origin of Species* established the theory of evolution.

2 Isambard Kingdom Brunel, the great engineer who developed bridges, trains and steamships.

3 Rowland Hill, who started the 'penny post' system which began in 1840.

4 Joseph Lister, who pioneered the use of antiseptics in surgery.

5 Thomas Huxley, a great biologist who upheld Darwin's theory of evolution.

6 Michael Faraday, a chemist and physicist who investigated the laws of electricity.

7 Herbert Spencer, a philosopher who believed in scientific methods and social progress.

The Motor Car

Farmer: "Pull up, you fool! The mare's bolting!"
Motorist: "So's the car!"

◀ This cartoon from *Punch* was entitled 'Brothers in Adversity.' At the end of the Victorian era, motor cars were appearing on the roads. A German, Karl Benz, produced the first petrol-driven vehicle for sale to the public in 1886.
On October 9, 1899, the first motorbus ran in London, and the first petrol-engined motor bicycle appeared in Britain in 1901.

Celebration

The family played an important part of Victorian social life, and the Royal Family was a model which many others came to revere. During Victoria's reign, affection for the monarchy dwindled and then soared.

The Queen had married her German cousin, Prince Albert of Saxe-Coburg-Gotha, in 1840. Albert devoted himself with energy and tact to his role. He came to influence events, without usurping the Queen's authority or upsetting her ministers. The royal couple had nine children who were to marry into the royal households of Europe.

Then, in 1861, Albert died of typhoid. The Queen withdrew from public life, devastated with grief. She went on to prolong her mourning to such an extent that many people lost sympathy. A cruel joker offered Buckingham Palace for let or sale as the occupant had gone out of business.

On the tenth anniversary of Albert's death, the Prince of Wales lay sick with fever—but he recovered. The Queen came out of seclusion, touched by the spontaneous joy of her people that she had been spared the loss of her son. She came to represent the power and glory of an expanding Empire. There were positive contributions she could make in memory of Albert by supporting science and the arts. The Golden Jubilee of 1887 was greeted with wild acclaim. Glittering processions passed through decorated streets lined with cheering crowds. All over the country, municipal corporations laid on celebrations.

Sixty years after her accession, she was still a purposeful, dominant little figure riding in an open carriage behind thousands of uniformed troops, and her people celebrated the Diamond Jubilee just as heartily.

The 'Widow of Windsor' had become a symbol of settled peace and prosperity, and when she died in 1901, it seemed that a whole era had come to an end.

▲ Girls dancing on Hampstead Heath on a Bank Holiday in 1890. When Victoria came to the throne, a working woman's life had been one of unrelieved drudgery. By the end of her reign there was something for women to celebrate. They still had no right to vote, but they did have the right to an education. Factory hours had been reduced, and new careers as nurses, teachers or typists were open to them. Hard-working milliners, housemaids and shop assistants could enjoy a day out in their best hats, and look forward to a better future.

▲ Men and women taking their partners to dance in the streets of Helston, Cornwall, on Flora Day. The Floral, or 'Furry' Dance still takes place on May 8th. Traditional dances such as morris and clog dancing added a distinctive character to regional celebrations.

▼ There were flags and Chinese lanterns to buy for the Golden Jubilee. Thousands of inscribed mugs were given to schoolchildren. The most amazing patriotic souvenir was a musical bustle which played the National Anthem when the woman wearing it sat down.

▲ Roasting a whole ox at Osney, Oxford, to celebrate the Golden Jubilee in 1887. The ox would be turned on a spit over the fire for most of the day. Notice the boy in the Union Jack cap in the bottom right-hand corner, and another behind the fence (top left).

Towns and villages held their own feasts and parties while the Royal pageantry flowed at Westminster. *The Times* reported, "No toast had been drunk oftener and with greater fervour and sincerity throughout the vast British Empire than that of "The Queen: God bless her..."

▲ Victoria, Queen of Great Britain and Empress of India, towards the end of her reign. Her son, later to be King Edward VII, is on her right. Her grandson, later to be King George V, is on her left. Her great-grandson, later to be King Edward VIII, is being restrained at her knee. Both our present Queen, Elizabeth II, and her consort Prince Philip, are great-great-grandchildren of Queen Victoria.

Fashion

Well-dressed women of the 1850's had tapering bodices with pointed waists to their dresses. The material curved over the hips into bell-shaped skirts of bouncy fullness.

To hold the skirt out, women came to wear devices called 'crinolines' instead of heavy petticoats. These were lightweight, hooped frames of cane or steel. By pulling a cord at the waist, the skirt could be lifted a few inches while out walking. Skirts with jackets or capes to match began to be worn, and this style developed into the tailored coat or skirt worn with a blouse.

In the 1870s, the shape changed. The front of the skirt was flatter, and full overskirts were concentrated at the back. They were supported by bustles, perhaps in a pleated train from the waist.

By the end of the century, the full and rounded contours were replaced by tubular shapes, worn with fine drapery clinging close. Bodices became more important, with trim waistcoats, and frothy 'jabots' of lace filling the V-shaped neckline.

Popular fabrics were chintz, flannel or cotton, twilled woollens and corded silks. Poplin, satin, velvet and gauze were used for ballgowns. None of these styles was complete without the right hat, parasol, gloves or mittens, shoes, bag and handkerchief.

Men's styles showed much less variety. Suits seemed to get darker and darker, and the waistcoat was the only garment to be decorated. Cravats got narrower as time went by, until the knotted tie replaced them. Boots were elastic-sided until button boots became fashionable in the 70s and 80s, only to be superseded by front laces.

No respectable man would be seen outdoors without a hat. At first, top hats were worn by people of all classes; later, bowlers, low-crowned felt hats and straw trilbys arrived.

▲ A working-class group in their Sunday best. Tight corseting moulded the figure inside the tailored clothes worn by the women. A child is dressed in a sailor suit, reflecting Britain's pride in her navy. The man, of course, wears a hat; in this case a small, peaked cap.

▲ A three piece suit of the 1850s. Trousers were narrow, strapped under the foot. 'Fancy' waistcoats were soon to go out of fashion.

▲ Leisure wear, especially for the country, allowed a shorter jacket of tweed, and a softer hat with a low crown.

▲ The crinoline of the 1850s. The word was used both for horsehair petticoats, and for the frames of steel or whalebone hoops which replaced them. Both had the effect of holding out the skirt, and both could be unmanageable in a crowded room or street.

▲ The bustle of the 1870s. Here, the fullness of the dress was pushed to the back, giving a 'cuirass' shape. It was achieved by a long corset and a steel-based pad, or 'jupon', of puffed horse-hair or merino; the bustle. This replaced earlier half-crinolines.

▲ By the 1890s, hoops and padding were giving way to simpler and more natural fashions in which it might even be possible to bicycle. Mrs Bloomer had tried to introduce trousered costumes in the 1850s, but was ridiculed at the time.

▼ Bathing costumes at the end of the century were tunic dresses to the knee, with sashes at the waist, and matching drawers showing below the knee. It was usual to wear stockings. Long hair was pinned up under a mob cap.

1900

Mourning customs demanded that a woman should wear black for months, or even years, after a loved one had passed away. This advertisement of 1881 shows that fashions for women in mourning had become big business and had little to do with genuine grief.

The Main Events

1851
The Great Exhibition was held at the Crystal Palace.
The first grants were made to evening schools.
Harriet Beecher Stowe published *Uncle Tom's Cabin.*
Singer produced the first practical sewing machine.

1852
Cholera; the third epidemic ravaged Britain.
Morse Code was used in telegraphy.
Tasmania ceased to be a convict settlement.
Livingstone set off to explore the Zambesi.

1853
Anaesthetics became widely accepted after chloroform helped Queen Victoria in childbearing.
Vaccination against smallpox was made compulsory.

1854
Britain entered the Crimean War. The battles of Alma, Balaclava and Inkerman, and the siege of Sebastopol took place.
Cheltenham Ladies' College was opened.
The Juvenile Offenders' Act was passed.

1855
A Committee of Enquiry was set up to examine the mismanagement of the Crimean War.
Florence Nightingale brought hygiene to nursing.
The first iron Cunard steamer crossed the Atlantic.
The tax on newspapers was abolished.

1856
The Crimean War ended with the Treaty of Paris.
Bessemer's process advanced steel production.
The Victoria Cross was instituted as an award for gallantry in action.

1857
The Indian Mutiny broke out.
The Hallé concerts began in Manchester.
South Kensington Museum was opened.

1858
The Indian Mutiny was suppressed; the British Crown took over powers from the East India Company.
Jews were admitted to Parliament, and M.P.'s property qualifications were ended.
Brunel's *Great Eastern* was launched.

1859
De Lesseps began work on the Suez Canal.
The first cottage hospital opened.
Darwin published his *Origin of Species.*
Samuel Smiles' *Self-help; How to Succeed in Life* appeared.

1860
Gladstone promoted Free Trade.
The British captured Peking.
The first English horse-drawn trams appeared.

1861
Albert, Prince Consort, died.
The American Civil War began; magazine rifles appeared.
Lancashire's cotton famine began.
Pasteur proposed his theory of germs.

1862
The Revised Code of Education set up the system of Payment by Results.
Bismarck came to power in Prussia.
Abraham Lincoln abolished slavery in America.

1863
The Prince of Wales (later Edward VII) married Alexandra of Denmark.

Rules for Association Football were laid down.
The Co-operative Wholesale Society was founded.
Charles Kingsley published *The Water Babies.*

1864
The Chimney Sweeps Act forbade the employment of children; but was ineffectual.
The Dale Dyke reservoir in Sheffield collapsed; about 250 people died.
The torpedo, and pasteurization, were invented.

1865
The American Civil War ended; President Lincoln was assassinated.
The Metropolitan Fire Service was set up.
Overarm bowling was permitted in cricket.
Lewis Carroll published *Alice in Wonderland.*

1866
Gladstone's Reform Bill was defeated; riots in Hyde Park.
Queensberry rules were adopted in boxing.
Dr Barnardo opened his home for waifs.

1867
Working men in towns got the vote.
Lister introduced carbolic antiseptic.
Unrest and violence flared in Ireland.
Trade unions were declared illegal.
Karl Marx published *Das Kapital.*

1868
Gangs Act forbade employment in farming of children under 8.
First Trade Union Congress was held in Manchester.
Disraeli became Prime Minister; resigned when the Liberals won the election.

1869
Wages in the iron industry were related to the selling price of iron.
Imprisonment for debt was abolished.
The Suez Canal was opened.
The first trans-continental railway was opened in the United States.

1870
Forster's Elementary Education Act set up school boards.
The Irish Land Act was passed; loans were granted to peasants to buy land, and they were given the right to compensation for eviction.
The $\frac{1}{2}$d post was introduced.

1871
Full legal recognition was given to trade unions.
Local government boards were created.
Edward Lear published *Nonsense Songs.*
Newnham College, Cambridge, was founded for women.
Stanley found Livingstone.

1872
The Ballot Act introduced voting in secret.
The Agricultural Workers' Union was founded by Joseph Arch.
Public houses were required to close at midnight in London and 10 pm in the country.

1873
The Ashanti War broke out, lasting till 1874.
There was an economic crisis with signs of industrial and agricultural depression.
Barbed wire was invented in the United States.
The first successful typewriter appeared.

1874
The Conservatives won the election; Disraeli became Prime Minister.
The Factory Act introduced a maximum 10 hour working day and raised the minimum age of child workers.
English lawn tennis began.

1875
Disraeli introduced social reforms; Public Health, Artisans' Dwellings, Sale of Food and Drugs and Climbing Boys Acts.

London's drainage system was completed.
Gilbert and Sullivan's partnership began with *Trial by Jury.*

1876
Bell's telephone, Edison's phonograph and Bissell's carpet sweeper were invented.
War broke out in the Balkans; Turks massacred Bulgarians.
The Plimsoll line was introduced to stop ships being overloaded.
Peaceful picketing during strikes was made legal.
School attendance was made compulsory.

1877
Victoria was proclaimed Empress of India.
Britain annexed the Transvaal.
Russia invaded Turkey.
Anna Sewell wrote *Black Beauty.*

1878
The Congress of Berlin settled the Eastern Question; Britain was to administer Cyprus.
The 'Red Flag' Act restricted the speed of mechanical road vehicles.
Electric street lighting began in London.
The C.I.D. was established.

1879
Swan and Edison independently produced the carbon filament incandescent electric light.
Electric railways were demonstrated.
The Zulu and Afghan wars broke out.
The Tay Bridge, longest in the world, collapsed.

1880
Ten thousand Irish evictions; boycotting began.
Gladstone won the election.
Irish Home Rulers obstructed parliamentary business.
The Transvaal Boers declared a republic.
Frozen meat was imported from Australia.

1881
Boer victories led to the Treaty of Pretoria in which Britain recognised Transvaal's independence.
The Irish Land Act set up courts to fix fair rents.
Punishment by flogging was abolished in the armed forces.

1882
The Phoenix Park murders took place in Dublin.
A British fleet bombarded Alexandria.
Fighting broke out in Egypt and the Sudan.
Cricket between England and Australia began the contest for the Ashes.

1883
The first skyscraper was built in Chicago, following the development of safety lifts by Otis.
General Gordon was sent to evacuate the Sudan.
Joseph Swan made the first artificial silk.

1884
The right to vote was granted to workers in agriculture.
Socialism grew under the influence of William Morris's Socialist League and the Fabian Society.
Maxim machine guns were developed.

1885
Khartoum fell; Gordon died.
Daimler developed lightweight, high-speed petrol engines in Germany.

1886
The Liberal Party split into Liberals and Unionists over the Irish Home Rule issue.
Hydro-electric installations were set up at the Niagara Falls.
The gas mantle was invented.

1887
The Golden Jubilee was celebrated.
The Coal Mines Regulation Act was passed; boys under 13 were not allowed underground.
Britain annexed Zululand.
Irish agitators attended a socialist meeting in Trafalgar Square; 'Bloody Sunday.'

88
nlop developed the pneumatic tyre.
e Kodak box camera appeared.
ack the Ripper' murders took place in London.
e Local Government Act set up county councils.
e matchgirls went on strike.

89
e London dockers went on strike for the
ockers' Tanner'.
Act was passed to prevent cruelty to children.

90
divorce case ruined the career of Parnell, the
sh Nationalist leader.
otion picture films were shown in New York.
e London-Paris telephone line opened.
e first 'tube' railway opened.

91
ir Hardie became the first Independent Labour
rty M.P.
ireless telegraphy was developed.
nan Doyle published The Adventures of
erlock Holmes.

92
adstone became Prime Minister for the fourth
d last time.
ned pineapple was introduced.
e first automatic telephone switchboard was
t up.

93
ere was a nationwide mining strike in Britain.
e Liverpool overhead electric railway was built.
pirin was introduced.

94
e Manchester Ship Canal was opened.
e Turbinia became the first steam turbine ship.

95
ntgen discovered X rays.
llette invented the safety razor.
anti-toxin for diphtheria was introduced.
e first motor car exhibition was put on in London.

96
e Red Flag Act was repealed, and the maximum
ed was raised to 14 mph.
art surgery was developed.
e first modern Olympic Games were held in
hens.

97
e Diamond Jubilee was celebrated.
e Workmen's Compensation Act increased
ployers' liability.
e monotype type-setting machine was invented.

98
e British under Kitchener defeated the Mahdi
d dervishes at the Battle of Omdurman.
erre and Marie Curie discovered radium.
e first zeppelin airship was built.

99
ar broke out between the British and Boers.
e White Star luxury liner SS Oceanic was
unched.
e first garden city was built at Letchworth.

00
e Boxer rebellion broke out in China.
dysmith and Mafeking were relieved during the
er War.
dbury established the Bournville Village Trust.

01
een Victoria died.
the Taff Vale case, it was judged that trade
ions could be sued as corporate bodies.
wntree published Poverty, a Study of Town
fe. The first Nobel prizes were awarded.
arconi transmitted wireless messages from
rnwall to Newfoundland.
e peace of Peking ended the Boxer rebellion.

▲ Sikh soldiers of the Punjab at the time of the Indian Mutiny in 1857. They did not join in the rebellion, but remained loyal to the British authorities.

▲ Scottish soldiers pose on the Great Sphinx in Egypt, 1882. Sir Garnet Wolseley had just defeated Arabi Pasha, leader of a mutiny against the Egyptian ruler.

▲ Boer soldiers in South Africa await a British attack. The Boer War continued after Queen Victoria's death, and did not end until 1902, in the reign of Edward VII.

Transport

For journeys over long distances, the second half of the 19th century was dominated by steam power. On land, the railways expanded rapidly. In 1852, there were 7,000 miles of track. By 1914, 23,000 miles of track were in use. Five million passengers travelled by rail in the 1870s, and the numbers went on increasing.

At sea, speedy clipper ships crossed the oceans under sail, but steamships were coming to rival them. Brunel's steamer *Great Britain* made the first Atlantic crossing in 1845, and developments followed rapidly. Paddle-wheels were replaced by screw propellors. Ships were made of iron instead of wood. At the turn of the century, Charles Parson's steam turbine engine made ocean crossings faster.

Steam boosted both passenger transport and merchant fleets. British shipping increased from 150 million tons in 1850 to 950 million tons in 1900.

For short distances and daily trips across town, the horse was still much used. The rich could take a hansom cab from door to door, while the less well-off rode in horse-drawn trams or horse omnibuses. Steam trams were tried in some cities, and after 1884 experiments were made with electric trams.

City streets thronged with horse-drawn vans and drays and carts on business. Passengers often got stuck in traffic jams. Then it was realised that people could be carried *below* street level. In 1862, a stretch of the Metropolitan Line was opened, as the first of London's underground railways. In 1890, electric trains replaced the steam engines which had made long tunnels a choking experience.

For working people, the bicycle brought a new freedom to travel anywhere, at any time. It became a cheap and popular form of personal transport.

▲ A horse-drawn omnibus. These appeared in 1829, as a solution for those who could not afford private carriages. By 1855, London horse omnibuses were carrying 20,000 passengers a day. They served the main business areas of the city, and the railway stations.

▼ Inside a horse omnibus. Rich and poor travelled together. There had been attempts to divide the seating into first class (an individual compartment), second class (four people sharing) and third class (seating on the roof). B one compartment for all meant lower fares.

▲ *The Railway Station* (1862) by William Frith. Paddington Station, shown here, was designed by Brunel. The picture portrays a mother seeing off her schoolboy son, a bridal group, and detectives making an arrest.

◄ Isambard Kingdom Brunel's gigantic steamship, the *Great Eastern* of 1858. Brunel himself was overworked and worn out with worry at the time of her launching.

▲ A 'penny-farthing'. These first, clumsy bicycles appeared in the 1870s, and demanded athletic skills from the rider. By 1886, a safety bicycle was on the market, and two years later pneumatic tyres appeared.

◄ A horse drawn coach. Such vehicles began to disappear because of competition from the railways. They were still needed in areas remote from rail routes, but roads deteriorated until the needs of motor cars were realised.

Who Was Who

Anderson, Elizabeth Garrett (1836-1917)
The first woman to qualify as a doctor in Britain, Miss Garrett had to overcome stiff opposition. She apprenticed herself to a doctor and outraged Edinburgh University by trying to attend anatomy lectures. With her father's help she fought legal battles to be allowed to take medical examinations. She qualified as a Doctor of Medicine in 1870, married, and was Dean of the London School of Medicine in 1883.

Bell, Alexander Graham (1847-1922)
Alexander Graham Bell was a Scotsman, born in Edinburgh and educated at Edinburgh University. He moved to Canada in 1870 because of ill health. Two years later, he opened a school in Boston for training teachers of the deaf. In 1876, he demonstrated an apparatus for transmitting sound by electricity; the telephone. Bell went on to develop phonographic devices, and to study the problems of mechanical flight.

Booth, William (1829-1912)
The founder of the Salvation Army, Booth came from a background of poverty. He was a Methodist, set up an East End mission, and began his war on drink and sin in 1865. In 1878, he organised his movement on military lines, taking campaigns into the worst slums, despite meeting violent rebuffs. Support for "General" Booth's crusade came with his book *In Darkest England and the Way Out*, published in 1890.

Brunel, Isambard Kingdom (1806-1859)
Brunel was an engineer who specialised in railway traction and bridges. He designed the Clifton suspension bridge, and, in 1833 was appointed engineer to the Great Western Railway. In his later years he devoted himself to steam navigation. He built the *SS Great Eastern*, the largest 19th century ship, having storage capacity for 2,500 miles of Atlantic cable. But the strain of building it made him ill; he died soon afterwards.

▲ W. E. Gladstone

▲ W. G. Grace

Carroll, Lewis (C. L. Dodgson) (1832-1898)
Lewis Carroll was the pen name of C. L. Dodgson, author of *Alice in Wonderland* (1865). He was a mathematician with a superb ability to write nonsense for the entertainment of children. Most Victorian children's books were supposed to point a moral, but there was growing appreciation for his tales for their own sake. *Alice*, illustrated by Tenniel, was followed by *Through the Looking Glass* and *The Hunting of the Snark*.

Darwin, Charles (1809-1882)
As a young scientist, Darwin set sail on the voyage of the *Beagle* in 1831, and came back with observations on the varieties of fossils and living animals which made him question Biblical accounts of the creation. He came to believe that humans had developed to their present state in a long struggle for survival. His great work *On the Origin of Species* was published in 1859. It caused a sensation and sold out on the first day of issue.

Dickens, Charles (1812-1870)
Dickens was a writer of novels which were outstandingly popular in their own time, and have remained so ever since. Characters and plots in his books often revolve around money, or the lack of it. His own childhood fortunes fluctuated. He knew prisons and factories first hand. His books first appeared in instalments, as his journalism rescued him from poverty. Later he made tours, and gave personal readings of famous passages.

Disraeli, Benjamin (1804-1881)
Disraeli began his career as a novelist whose books showed concern for the divisions between rich and poor in Britain. Later, as a politician and Prime Minister, he attempted to make remedies. He was a Conservative who believed in social reform and the building of the Empire. Shrewd and business-like on the nation's behalf, he was popularly known as "Dizzy". The Queen adored him, and created him Earl of Beaconsfield.

Doyle, Arthur Conan (1859-1930)
The young Conan Doyle was a doctor who began writing to support himself when his medical practice was slow to attract patients. Writing from Southsea, too poor to buy an existing practice, he created the character of Sherlock Holmes. His fictitious amateur detective brought him more success than he expected, and Holmes's scientific methods, with deduction by logical analysis, were to be adopted by the police.

Edison, Thomas Alva (1847-1931)
Edison was the inventor of over a thousand patented ideas which were to transform life in the late 19th century. Yet he had only attended school for three months in his life, and began earning his living as a newsboy. Born in America, Edison made the Bell telephone a practical concern, invented his own phonograph, and developed with Swan the electric carbon filament lamp, which was the origin of the modern light bulb.

Gladstone, William Ewart (1809-1898)
Gladstone was leader of the Liberal party for nearly a quarter of a century, and Prime Minister four times. At first, he had intended to enter the Church, and his religious sense added zeal to his political career. He joined the Tories under Peel but later switched parties to join Palmerston's Liberal ministry. His main interests were free trade, reform of the legal system, education, the army, and the problems of Ireland.

Gordon, Charles George (1833-1885)
Gordon was a military hero who also gave help to the children of the poor. He served in the Crimean War and in China and brought peace to the Sudan before retiring with honour. He was then returned to the Sudan to supervise the evacuation of troops threatened by the Mahdi's revolt. Besieged in Khartoum, Gordon was killed before help arrived. His death horrified the nation and the Government was blamed for the delay.

▲ Benjamin Disraeli

ace, William Gilbert (1848-1915)
is great cricketer was also a Doctor of Medicine.
e scored 54,896 runs in first class cricket, and
1876 made 400 not out. W. G. Grace was the
ost important figure in making the game a
tional institution. He also laid down several
tting and bowling techniques. He took 2,876
ckets in a career of nearly 50 years. His last
st class match was in 1908, when he was
id to be "60 years young".

ardie, James Keir (1856-1915)
eir Hardie was the founder of the Independent
bour Party from which the modern Labour Party
veloped. A Scot, born into a poor and
ercrowded household, he worked in a coal mine
fore he was ten. He grew up to be active in the
cottish Miners' Federation. In the late 1880s, he
allenged the idea that workers should be
presented in Parliament by either of the two
isting parties, and stood as the first Labour
ndidate in Britain.

ster, Joseph (1827-1912)
ord Lister was the pioneer of antiseptic surgery.
e came from a Quaker family, and was received
to the Royal College of Surgeons. He was
esent at the first operation performed with
aesthetic, and realised that although
nconscious patients now gave surgeons more
ne, septic wounds could still be fatal. He
veloped antiseptic routines after 12 years of
search. Lister is now remembered as one of the
thers of modern medicine.

vingstone, David (1813-1873)
missionary in central Africa, Livingstone explored
e course of the Zambesi River and the sources
the Nile. Three great expeditions took him into
e heart of the continent. At one time he was
esumed missing, but an expedition led by
. M. Stanley discovered him on the shore of
ke Tanganyika in 1871. Stanley later worked
r one of his aims, which was to suppress the
rab slave trade.

David Livingstone

Morris, William (1834-1896)
An artist and poet, Morris revolutionized
Victorian taste in furnishings and interior
decorating. He manufactured his own designs with
with a group of friends, and in 1877 began a lecture
tour. Moving through industrial areas and repelled
by their ugliness, he became a fervent socialist.
His writings turned more and more towards
encouraging visions of a social state in which
everyone shared creative labour.

▲ Florence Nightingale

Nightingale, Florence (1820-1910)
Florence Nightingale was the founder of
professional nursing and a pioneer of hospital
reform. She had to oppose her family's wishes in
order to become a nurse. She fought to improve
conditions during the Crimean War, and
afterwards received a fund of £50,000. This she
used to set up nursing colleges in England. She
was, above all, a gifted administrator, and spent
the rest of her life establishing good nursing
standards.

Ruskin, John (1819-1900)
Ruskin was a writer and social reformer. He
travelled widely, developing as an artist and art
critic, with a particular interest in architecture.
He disliked being labelled as a socialist, but
proposed schemes for full employment and social
services for the poor and aged which attracted
the label to him. As Professor of Fine Art at
Oxford, he took his students roadmaking.

Smiles, Samuel (1812-1904)
Smiles was the author of *Self-help* a best seller
which ran to over a quarter of a million copies
and was translated into most European and
Asiatic languages. He believed in making the most
of leisure hours, and in the thrifty management of
money. He came from a small but scholarly
Scottish home, qualified as a doctor, but finding

no job turned to editing a newspaper in Leeds.
He supported education, libraries and
co-operatives.

Tennyson, Alfred (1809-1892)
Tennyson's first important work was published
when he was 23, and for ten years he made a
reputation; but no money. Then, at the age of
only 33, he was granted a Civil List pension and
was able to write without fear of poverty to the
end of his long life. The Victorians loved the
descriptiveness and occasional melancholy of
Maud, Idylls of the King and his later poetic
dramas. He was made Poet Laureate in 1850.

Terry, Ellen Alicia (1847-1928)
Ellen Terry made her first appearance on the stage
when she was only nine (as a boy in *The
Winter's Tale*). In 1875, she played Portia in
The Merchant of Venice and won immediate
acclaim. She went on to become the most famous
actress on the English stage. In 1878, the actor
Henry Irving became manager of the Lyceum
theatre and engaged her as his leading lady. Their
great acting partnership lasted for 13 years.

Victoria, Queen and Empress (1819-1901)
Coming to the throne at the age of 19, Victoria
was influenced in her early years by her Prime
Minister, Lord Melbourne. Later she came to play
her role with greater personal authority. After
Prince Albert's death in 1861, her lonely royal
duties occupied her more and more. Her happiest
hours were spent at her estate in Balmoral, in the
company of Albert's plain-speaking Highland
servant, John Brown.

▲ Queen Victoria with John Brown

Wells, Herbert George (1866-1946)
H. G. Wells began his career at the age of 14 as a
draper's apprentice. He ran away, and tried
several other jobs before winning a scholarship
to study biology. Poor and dissatisfied as a
teacher of science, he turned to journalism. In
1895, he wrote his first novel, *The Time Machine*.
It was an immediate success and was swiftly
followed by *The Island of Doctor Moreau*.

Prize Cottages

In the early 19th century, labourers' dwellings had been thrown up at tremendous speed, without concern for comfort, safety or hygiene. But during the second half of the 19th century, Victorian architects began to experiment more and more with 'model housing' for working people; sensible and solidly built dwellings which would, nevertheless, be within the reach of the average wage-earner.

L. M. Fitzgerald was one such architect. He considered that improving working people's lives by preaching temperance and passing laws which compelled children to go to school was 'beginning at the wrong end.' First, the labourer's family must have a dry, comfortable home. What was the point of sending children home to dirt and misery? Was it surprising if a father fled from the one squalid room where his family 'huddled together like beasts' to the comfort of an inn?

In 1883, an Irish MP held a com-petition for architects, to find who coul design the best cottage which could b built for under £75. Fitzgerald wo his pair of cottages with their ou building costing £71/5/- each.

The pair were designed as two, inter locking, L-shaped cottages. Fitzgeral had concentrated on ways of providin extra comfort at no extra cost. F cheerfulness, economy, and neigh bourly help in times of illness, dwelling should be in pairs near the road, with southerly aspect. Sites should be war and dry, but near spring water. Cup boards built into the thickness kitchen walls cost no more, well-line flues retained heat and saved fuel.

Fitzgerald's aims were both idealisti and practical. He stressed the labourer right to a decent home. But he als pointed out that it was much cheape for Poor Law Unions to pay interest o loans for healthy housing than to main tain families driven into the workhous by ill health.

▼ The Villiers Stuart Prize Cottages. L. M. Fitzgerald's designs are shown below. The main accommodation for two families under a slate roof cost £105. In addition, each family needed a privy, a store and a piggery with a loft for fowls. These cost an extra £37 10/–. The total cost was thus £142 10/–, or £71 5/– each.

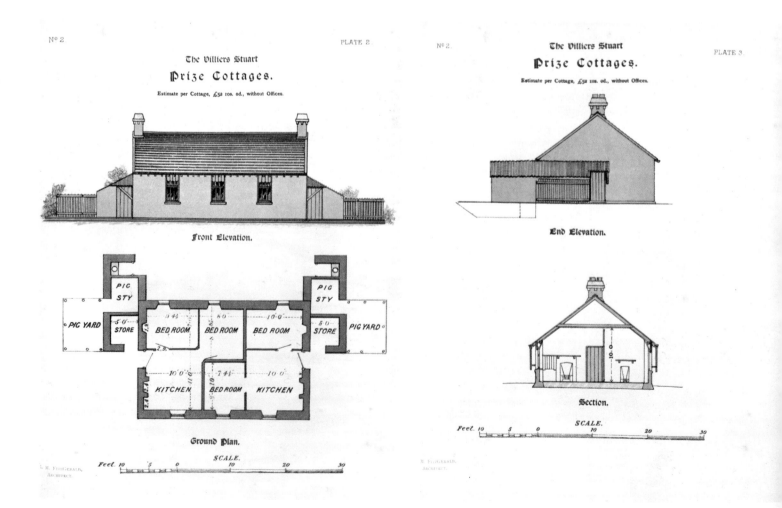

An artist's reconstruction of the prize cottages as they might have looked.

The judges were surprised to see a design on the floor only, for most labouring families used lofts for accommodation. But Fitzgerald explained that carrying the ceiling into the roof gave much needed air space. He pointed out that a bedroom in the loft, usually reached by a ladder, was dangerous to children. It was also difficult to clean, and so contributed to ill health.

The design was neat and compact and the judges approved. The cottages are hardly spacious by modern standards, however. Imagine the problems of a large family of six or more.

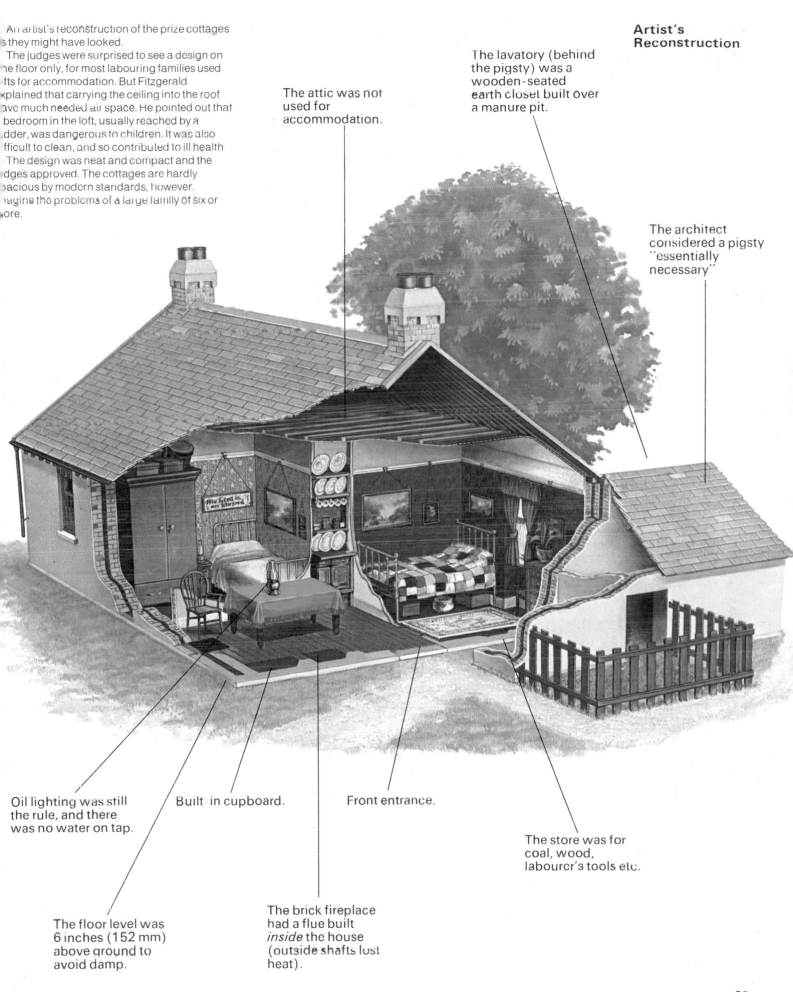

The attic was not used for accommodation.

The lavatory (behind the pigsty) was a wooden-seated earth closet built over a manure pit.

The architect considered a pigsty "essentially necessary"

Oil lighting was still the rule, and there was no water on tap.

Built-in cupboard.

Front entrance.

The store was for coal, wood, labourer's tools etc.

The floor level was 6 inches (152 mm) above ground to avoid damp.

The brick fireplace had a flue built *inside* the house (outside shafts lost heat).

The Army

Incompetent army leadership was revealed during the Crimean War. Britain entered in 1854, without proper organisation. Fodder for cavalry horses was left behind, and thousands of soldiers died of fever or unattended wounds. The famous Charge of the Light Brigade was really the result of confused commands. And once, a consignment of boots arrived at the front; for left feet only!

In India in 1857, the Hindu soldiers mutinied, believing the officers' orders conflicted with the Hindu religion.

Reforms came at last in 1871. Wealthy young men were no longer allowed to buy posts in the army. Officers now had to train as professionals, and were promoted on merit. Recruits were also enlisted to build up a trained reserve.

Britain's real military strength lay in advanced weaponry. In operations against Zulus, Afghans, Dervishes and Ashantis, the British were often out-numbered but still won the day. Tale of such encounters thrilled schoolboy as when two lieutenants with 80 me beat off 3,000 Zulus in the Defence Rorke's Drift (1879).

A new phrase was coined in honou of Sir Garnet Wolseley, whose skill as general retrieved mistakes made b politicians and other leaders. 'It wi be all Sir Garnet,' said troops in th camps (and nannies in nurseries a home) meaning that even disasters ca be remedied. But there was one disaste which Wolseley could not avert. I 1884, he was sent to rescue Genera Gordon, under siege in Khartoum Through no fault of his own, he arrive too late. Gordon was dead and h troops were massacred.

Twelve years after this famous even Kitchener arrived in the area with ne weapons, and troops in khaki (whic showed up less than red or blue). Th British flag was hoisted high on th building where Gordon had died.

▼ A photographic van during the Crimean War. Until mid-century, newspapers seldom carried pictures. When papers started sending war artists and photographs to the front line, the public at home was kept better informed. Battle scenes were often reproduced as engravings, made from the sketches or photographs.

▼ Soldiers in the Crimea relaxing at the front. They look cheerful enough in this photograph, but most were badly fed and ill-equipped to face the bitter cold. Hundreds died of cholera, and all medical supplies were inadequate.

▲ William Russell was war correspondent of *The Times*. His reports from Crimea were relayed by telegraph. He told of the troops' sufferings, of the la of transport, and how lives were being sacrificed through inefficiency.

◀ A Diamond Jubilee tribute to the 'Queen and Empress'. It suggests how much the British Empire relied on its army and navy. Nearly a quarter of the world population belonged to the Empire.

▲ Military athletics at Sandhurst in 1881. Apart from physical training, professional qualifications were required in tactics, military law, fortification and topography.

▼ Storming a *kopje* in the Boer War. A *kopje* was a hillock, and occupying high ground gave a strategic advantage.

The Steam Train

Stirling Single No. 1, 1870

Boiler

Chimney

Smoke box door

Handrail

Sandbox

Vacuum brake connection

Buffer

Lamp

Dumb iron

Cylinder

Crosshead

Coupling

Piston rod

Brake sho

Nothing symbolised Victorian pride in engineering more than the steam train, and few locomotives were more impressive than the Stirling Single. Stirling engines hauled the great *Flying Scotsman* express, perhaps the most famous of all the great trains of the Victorian Age.

'Singles' were engines which had just one pair of driving wheels. These were large and powerful and rose up on either side of the boiler. The wide diameter of the driving wheels gave the locomotive its speed.

There were developments in coach design. The 'Cheap Trains Act' of 1844 instituted 'Parliamentary' penny-a-mile trains once a day; before, third-class passengers had been carried in open goods trucks at $1\frac{1}{2}$d a mile. For wealthier passengers, Pullman coaches and dining cars made journeys much more comfortable. Queen Victoria herself travelled to Balmoral in a luxurious private carriage built for her in 1869.

Speed, safety and comfort benefited the railway companies as much as the public. Between 1845 and 1890, first-class receipts doubled. Third-class receipts, from passengers paying a penny a mile, multiplied by 32!

▼A first class coach of 1877, provided by the Great Northern Railway for the East Coast Joint Stock. It was mounted on a six-wheeled underframe unlike earlier four-wheelers.

Coaches like this were the first to have side corridors, though there were no connecting door to other carriages. At each end was a lavatory, one for ladies, the other for gentlemen.

Great Northern Railway Coach, 1877

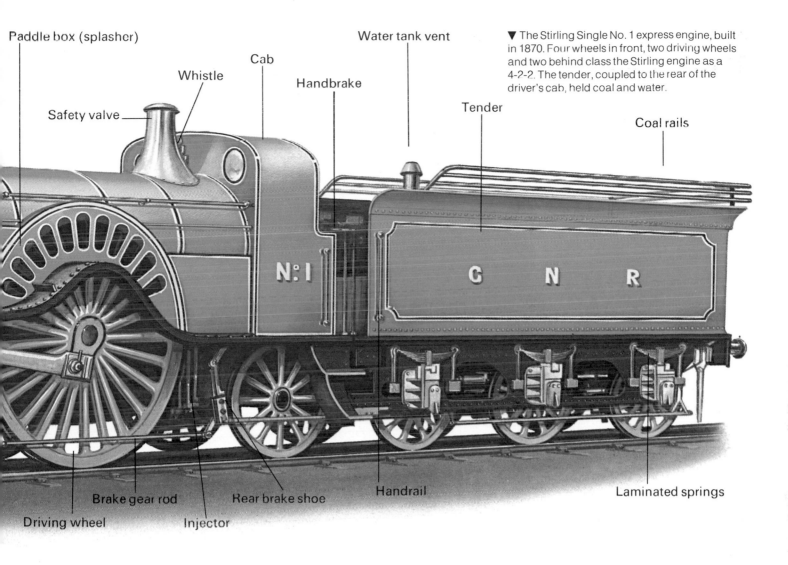

Paddle box (splasher)

Whistle

Safety valve

Cab

Handbrake

Water tank vent

Tender

Coal rails

▼ The Stirling Single No. 1 express engine, built in 1870. Four wheels in front, two driving wheels and two behind class the Stirling engine as a 4-2-2. The tender, coupled to the rear of the driver's cab, held coal and water.

N°I

C N R

Brake gear rod

Rear brake shoe

Handrail

Laminated springs

Driving wheel

Injector

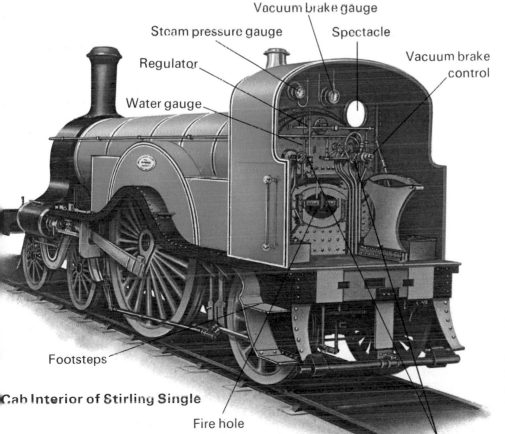

Vacuum brake gauge

Steam pressure gauge

Spectacle

Regulator

Vacuum brake control

Water gauge

Footsteps

Cab Interior of Stirling Single

Fire hole

Injector controls for boiler feed water

◀ The cab interior of a Stirling Single. This is a slightly later model than the one above. The slots on the splashers are covered. Automatic vacuum brakes have been fitted, working on all the wheels along the train. The driver would earn about £2 a week.

Advantages

The social advantages of steam engines were not limited to passenger transport. Food and milk arrived in town centres fresher than ever before. It had once cost several shillings to send a letter from London to Scotland, now the railways made communications cheaper and the penny post possible. A general parcel post was added to the mail service in 1883.

The expansion of railway goods services created thousands of clerical jobs. British engineering experience enabled her to export locomotives and rolling stock abroad. Demand for coal, iron and steel increased steadily. The age of steam was noisy and dirty; but it was undeniably prosperous.

Projects

Reading list

Allen, Eleanor, *Victorian Children,*
   Adam and Charles Black, 1973.
Avery, Gillian, *Victorian People,* Collins 1970.
British Broadcasting Corporation,
   Eminently Victorian, 1974.
Harrison, Molly, *Home Inventions,* Usborne,
   1975.
Hibbert, Christopher, *Social History of
   Victorian Britain,* Angus and Robertson,
   1975.
Hugget, Frank E., *A Day in the Life of a
   Victorian Farmworker,* George Allen and
   Unwin, 1972.
Poulton, Richard, *Victoria, Queen of a
   Changing Land,* World's Work, 1975.
Priestley, J. B., *Victoria's Heyday,* Heinemann,
   1972.
Reader, W. J., *Victorian England,* Batsford,
   1973.
Rooke, Patrick, *The Age of Dickens,* Wayland,
   1970.
Then and There series (several titles),
   Longman, 1970s.
Turner, Michael R., *The Parlour Songbook,*
   Michael Joseph, 1972.
Unstead, R.J., *Age of Machines,* Macdonald
   Educational, 1974.
William-Ellis, Annabel and William Stobbs,
   Victorian England, Blackie, 1969.

▲ The village band of Corby Pole, Northampton.
They probably enjoyed playing rousing marches.

▲ Beach performers at Southsea in the 1890s.
Seaside concert parties sang minstrel songs.

Songs We Used To Sing

Popular songs of the period reveal much about Victorian life. Gilbert and Sullivan's comic operas, for example, are full of topical jokes. *HMS Pinafore* made fun of W. H. Smith's rise in politics. *Iolanthe* poked fun at the House of Lords, and the *Gondoliers* at social change: 'When everyone is somebody, then no-one's anybody!'

Princess Ida mocked the idea of women going to university. In the *Mikado* evil-doers are punished by being made to 'ride on a buffer in Parliamentary trains,' or attend 'classical Monday Pops' (cultural concerts for workers). Songs from these operas reveal not only some of the history of the time, but also the Victorian taste for good (and bad) puns.

Parlour songs included many sentimental ballads about working children. The following verse describes a flower girl:
"*Underneath the gaslight's glitter
Stands a little fragile girl,
Heedless of the night winds bitter
As they round about her whirl,
While the hundreds pass unheeding
In the evening's waning hours,
Still she cries with tearful pleading,
'Won't you buy my pretty flowers?'*"
Temperance songs often stressed the plight of a drunkard's family, as in the chorus of *The Drunkard's Child:*
"*Please sell no more drink to my father
It makes him so strange and so wild,
Heed the prayer of my heart-broken mother
And pity the poor drunkard's child.*"
In contrast, patriotic songs tended to be robust, like this song of 1877 which expressed Britain's determination to beat the Russian 'Bear':
"*We don't want to fight,
But, by Jingo! if we do,
We've got the ships
We've got the men
We've got the money too.*"
This song became so famous that a new word entered the English language: 'Jingoism,' meaning over-hearty patriotism.

Here are some simple recipes from Mrs Beeton's famous *Book of Household Management*.

Lemonade

Ingredients: $\frac{1}{2}$ pint cold water, the juice of one lemon, $\frac{1}{4}$ teaspoonful of bicarbonate of soda, caster sugar to taste.

Strain the juice of the lemon into the water, sweeten to taste, stir in the bicarbonate of soda and drink while the mixture is in an effervescing state (while it is 'fizzy').

Baking powder bread

Ingredients: 1 lb of flour, $\frac{1}{2}$ oz. of baking powder, 2 teaspoonsful of salt, $\frac{1}{2}$ pint of milk.

Mix salt and baking powder into the flour on a board, then make a hollow in the centre of the flour, pour in almost all the milk, and knead as quickly as possible and with very little handling into a nice, light dough. Divide it into loaves, shape them up, wash over with a little milk and bake in a quick (hot) oven.

'It is very necessary to get the loaves into the oven with the greatest dispatch as the baking powder soon loses its virtue,' warned Mrs Beeton. Bear in mind that her suggested baking time ($\frac{3}{4}$ hour) would apply to one of the kitchen ranges of her day. In a modern oven, 20 minutes is enough.

If you want to experience a meal given to a Victorian invalid or workhouse inmate, here is Mrs Beeton's recipe for gruel.

Gruel

Ingredients: oatmeal, salt, water.

Mix a tablespoonful of fine oatmeal with a little cold water taken from one pint. Boil the rest of the water, pour in the wet oatmeal, and stir together until boiling. Simmer gently for half an hour. Add a pinch of salt.

That would do for a workhouse inmate! For an invalid, add sugar, nutmeg, ginger, butter or cream.

A Monday Menu

Mrs Beeton gave menus for family meals throughout the day, all year round. Here is one for an ordinary Monday dinner in autumn: Lobster soup; Whiting soufflé; Stewed pigeons with rissole potatoes; Saddle of mutton, cauliflower and boiled potatoes; Vanilla soufflé or fruit in jelly; Anchovy fritters.

▲ Mrs Beeton's classic guide to the smooth running of a home was published in 1861. It was intended for middle-class women, giving advice on the treatment of servants and setting out rules of etiquette. Hints on every job, from cleaning tortoiseshell to taking the creak out of a pair of boots were included. It was a best seller for years.

▲ Packing Cambridge Lemonade at Chivers' factory in 1894. The mass production of food and drinks took away some of the burden from cooks and housewives.

▲ A bread oven near Prudhoe. Many families made their own bread.

Projects

String telephone

Pierce hole in base of tin

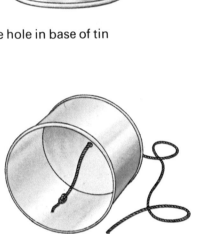

Knot string

Keep string taut

Pinhole camera

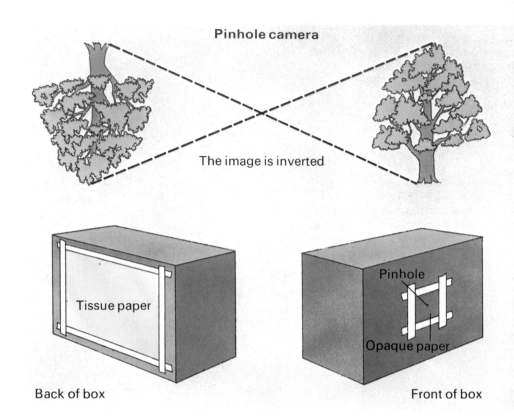

The image is inverted

Tissue paper

Back of box

Pinhole

Opaque paper

Front of box

Making a string telephone

The telephone, invented in 1876, was one of the marvels of Victorian ingenuity. You can make a simple telephone which works on the same principle as a real one. All you need are two tin cans (or cardboard cups or yoghurt cartons) and a length of string. The string can be as little as 7 metres, or as much as 30 metres long.

Make a hole in the bottom of each tin. Pass one end of the piece of string through each hole and knot it tightly. Now stretch the string out in a straight line, keeping it taut.

As you speak into the tin, its base vibrates in the same way as the diaphragm of a telephone. The vibrations pass out along the string to the base of the other tin. This in turn vibrates, and the listener at the end can hear what you say.

Making a pinhole camera

When light rays pass through a narrow opening, they cause an image to appear upside down on the other side. This is the principle of the camera. Victorian photographers saw an inverted image when they took a picture.

Take a cardboard box and remove the ends. Cover one end with transparent tissue or greaseproof paper, stretching it tight. Cover the other end with opaque paper (paper which does not let light through), or with metal foil. Make a pinhole in the opaque paper. Cover your head, and all except the front of the camera, with a dark cloth, like a Victorian photographer. Point the pinhole at a window, or other bright light. You should see the image appear upside down on the back of the box. In a real camera, this would be the film, coated with a substance to fix the image.

MAKING A ZOETROPE

Making the drum

The open-topped drum of a zoetrope can be made from card. For the cylindrical sides, cut a length of card 58 cms long and 17 cms wide. Rule parallel lines 2 cms in from each long edge. From the top line, draw down eleven lines, 5 cms long and 5 cms apart. You will find you have cms of card left over at one end; this is to overlap the join when you make this piece into a cylinder.

Draw zig-zag lines from the bottom 2 cm line to the edge. This piece should now look like figure 1. Cut the vertical 5 cm lines to a width of about 5 mms. These make the slits through which you will view the strip. (A Stanley knife is better than scissors for this job). Also cut out the small triangles of card at the bottom edge.

To make the base (*figure 2*), use compasses to draw a circle with a 9 cm radius, on card. (You can simply draw around a 45 rpm 'single' record). Cut out the circle and punch a hole in the centre.

Now bend the rectangular piece of card round to make a cylinder. Glue or tape the short edges together, making sure that the overlapping card does not obscure a slit. Fold the triangular pieces at the bottom edge inwards, and glue them down to the circular base (*figure 3*). For added effect, you can now paint the whole drum black.

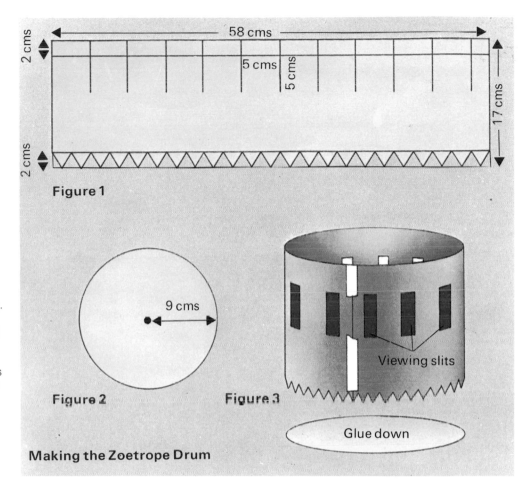

Figure 1

Figure 2

Figure 3

Viewing slits

Glue down

Making the Zoetrope Drum

Making the strips

Cut out eleven pieces of paper 5 cms wide by 8 cms tall. Stack them neatly on top of one another. Draw a simple figure in pencil on the first sheet, pressing down hard; it is better to draw a solid figure than a 'stick man'. For this example we are using a man with a bowler hat (*figure 4*).

You should find that there is an impression of your figure on the second sheet (*figure 5*). Use this impression as a guide, drawing in the figure again, but making a slight alteration to one limb (*figure 6*). Repeat this method on the remaining nine sheets to show a whole sequence of movement; in our example the figure is raising his hat. Colour in the figures and glue them down on a strip of paper 58 cm long and 8 cm high. (*figure 7*). Bend the strip round and join the ends, with the figures facing inwards (*figure 8*). Place the strip inside the drum, below the slits.

To view the moving picture, put the zoetrope on any pivot on which it can spin freely. For the best effects, try it on a record-player turntable at different speeds. Watch through the slits in the side of the drum, and try shining a torch from above.

You can add to your stock of picture strips, or experiment with a bigger zoetrope. You can try one with slits closer together, or with larger or smaller pictures.

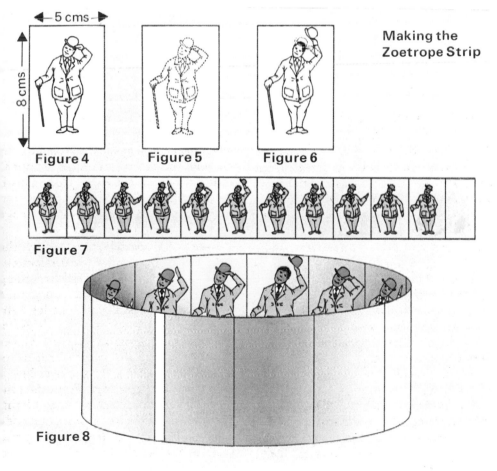

Making the Zoetrope Strip

Figure 4

Figure 5

Figure 6

Figure 7

Figure 8

Index